Listening to God

An inspirational truth
for each day
to bless or inspire you

Mary M. Chase

Listening to God

Mary M. Chase

ISBN 1516858417
Copyright © 2015
Mary M. Chase

Oklahoma City, Oklahoma

ALL RIGHTS RESERVED

NO PART OF THIS BOOK MAY BE REPRODUCED IN ANY FORM, BY PHOTOCOPYING OR BY ANY ELECTRONIC OR MECHANICAL MEANS, INCLUDING INFORMATION STORAGE OR RETRIEVAL SYSTEMS, WITHOUT PERMISSION IN WRITING FROM THE COPYRIGHT OWNER.

Printed in the USA

From the Author

This book of devotional thoughts is the result of my own search to sense God's presence each day and glean whatever He says to my heart. It is my desire that each child of God sets aside some time with Him daily, for I believe He desires our fellowship and to feel we know Him personally. While reading the Scripture in these quiet moments you will sense His warm presence and enjoy a fresh awakening, a renewal of mind, soul, and body, for in solitude God speaks in a still small voice to the heart through the Word.

We each seek inner peace and contentment in life, but too often we rush through our days letting these comforts escape by not sitting quietly with Him daily. I learned from Psalm 91 that King David also sat abiding in His presence, and tells us, "He who dwells in the secret place of the Most High shall abide under the shadow of the Almighty. I will say He is my refuge and my fortress; in Him I will trust." Even our Lord set the example for us, He often withdrew from the crowds to sit in solitude with the Father.

For me it has been a long journey since that hot August night, when as a young teenage girl I lifted myself from an old wooden altar at a small country church revival meeting held under an old fashioned brush arbor. I've never doubted that the "someone' who had sat with me in the old plum tree in Grandpa's orchard comforting me as a troubled child was the same Someone who had beckoned to me at this revival meeting to come unto Him as my Redeemer. The Lord has walked with me step by step since that time.

Now as I gaze back I see many milestones of faith as I've traveled each day praying: "0 Lord, show me Your ways. Teach me Your paths. Lead me in Your truth. Teach me for you are the God of my salvation and on You I wait all the day." Psalm 25:4-5. Since that 1936 beginning I've found each sunrise to be a new fresh start, and ready to serve Him, but I've daily needed His wisdom and guidance regarding my life's decisions. I constantly remind myself that God planned each day of this journey, and I am not to rush ahead in unwise decisions. "...for in Your book they were all written, the days fashioned for me, when as yet there were none of them." Psalm 139:16.

I can trace God's hand throughout my life, even though I've strayed at times, but always felt drawn back to Him. I have also traversed some hard times I did not understand, but I knew for some reason it must be in God's plan for me. In spite of it all through these many years, I've desired this close relationship with Him.

I pray these daily mini-thoughts from my own experience will lead you also into a daily fellowship with Him. You will be blessed as He reveals Himself in the stillness of these few quiet moments you spend with Him. The one thing that I've prayed daily through the years is that all those about me will see God's love and grace in my life.

Meditations

M.M.C.

Oct 28-15

Listen to Hear My Voice

Have you ever been asked, "How does God speak to you? We know Satan puts thoughts in one's mind, so how can we know it Is God's voice? Well, first, Satan gives easy answers and feel good ideas as solutions. God does not speak verbally to us, but sometimes ideas pop in mind that line up with God's Word that I could never have thought to speak or write myself. He speaks through the Word, but is not limited in how He speaks to our hearts.

Psalm 139:17-18 says that His thoughts toward us are more in number that the sands of the sea. David tells God in Psalm 73:24, "You guide me with Your counsel..." also "Let the morning bring me word of your unfailing love... show me the way I should go..." Psalm 143:8.

God speaks to our receptive hearts. If you sit quietly with God, your heart will hear His still, small voice. It says in Isaiah 28:23: "Listen and hear My voice, pay attention and hear what I say." Isaiah 30:21 "Whether you turn to the right or to the left, your ears will hear a voice behind you, saying this is the way, walk in it." It's the Living Word that speaks and directs us.

A Bible Hero

Paul tops my list. Saul of Tarsus was a brutal man determined in stamping out this movement of Jesus, for he considered it against God. He became a cold-blooded murderer who thought he was doing God's will, but God reached his heart by letting him witness Stephen's death who courageously died praising God. Saul, a religious man of the Law watched this holy man die. You know the story of how he left on the road to Damascus with orders from the high priest to bring every believer found back to be killed in Jerusalem, but on the road Saul was blinded by a light and a voice, "Saul, Saul, why are you persecuting Me?" Saul loved God faithfully and in response. He ask, "Who are you, LORD?" The answer "I am Jesus, whom you are persecuting…" His famous question, "LORD, what do You want me to do?" God sent Ananias to him saying, "Saul is a chosen vessel of mine – he will bear My name to the Gentiles. Go to him for I have blinded him."

Paul tells us in Galatians 1:16-17 that God "revealed His Son in Me that I might preach to the Gentiles…" Today we thank Paul for bringing the gospel to our Gentile world.

Faithful to the End

The book of Jeremiah is a life journal of one of the greatest prophet in the Bible in my estimation. He was called the Preacher and his message was nothing but gloom and doom for God's people, and they didn't want to hear it. They ridiculed him on every hand, but God told Jeremiah that His hand was on him even before he was born. Jeremiah in 1: 5, "Before I formed you in the womb I knew you; before you were born I sanctified you, ordained you a prophet to the nations." If there was ever a profile of endurance to the end, it's Jeremiah. For forty years his message was judgment and his listeners didn't want to hear it. He had no wife or children of his own. Jeremiah 16:1 "The word of the Lord came me say, "You shall not take a wife, nor shall you have sons and daughters in this place." This nation of Israel finally felt God's judgment in bondage, as Jeremiah saw God's total faithfulness.

As Jeremiah wept over Jerusalem for rejection; we see history repeated as Jesus seated on the Mount of Olives weeping over those who rejected Him. "O Jerusalem, Jerusalem, the one who kills the prophets sent to them. I wanted to gather your children together, as a hen gathers her chicks under her wing, but you were not willing." He wept as the prophet Jeremiah wept.

New Creatures

We enjoy seeing any form of transformation, whether it's an ugly duckling to a beautiful swan, or the Phoenix rising from ashes. The essential part of any story is transforming a problem into a satisfactory ending. The same is true with Christianity. "...You must be born again" John 3:7, to be transformed is the central message of the gospel. We can clean up our lives, but nothing counts if the inner being is not changed into a new creation in Christ, which changes our thinking and ways of living. We live in the devil's kingdom and must deal with him, but we have help from the Holy Spirit in us in order to overcome.

We have great examples in the Bible of transformed lives. First I think of Mary Magdalene, who lived in the gutter, and became a devout worshiper; Paul, who was Saul the murderer transformed with one encounter with the Lord. We have witnessed many lives change by redemption, and became new creatures in Christ. In II Corinthians 5:17 "...if anyone is in Christ, he is a new creation..." This spiritual transformation occurs in the inner man when a person accepts Christ as his Redeemer. It's a new existence, but the new nature needs cultivation to live a victorious life. When you see a true follower of Christ, you're witnessing a transformed life.

God's Leadership

"Thus says the Lord to His anointed, to Cyrus….that you may know that I am the Lord, the God of Israel who calls you by name. I will go before you and make the crooked places straight. I will break in pieces the gates of bronze and will cut the bars of iron. I will give you the treasures of darkness and hidden riches of secret places, so you can know that I am the Lord". Isaiah 1-3. What's remarkable is these words were spoken to a pagan, King Cyrus of Persia, who had just conquered Babylon, and held God's people in bondage. God called this Gentile king His anointed, which in this case God used a pagan king to do His will. The Word says in verse 13 "I will raise up Cyrus…I will make his ways straight. He will rebuild my city and set my exiles free…" This happened. Read it again. God also makes these promises to us, His people. Just hear what His words say to us. He desires to walk with us on life's journey. We come to intersections and are to seek our Guide and follow Him. He becomes a part of our identity. His says "I will go before you…"

Junctions in life appear as two ways, we can't clearly see either path ahead. God does not give us a road map, but wants us to trust Him as He navigates life with us.

Light Available

Every time I look at the lighted pole in my back yard casting light into the dark corners, I'm reminded of the promise of light throughout God's word. I still remember the oil lamps used when I lived with my grandparents on the farm. The light was warm in color and cast shadows on the wall, but there was just enough light for our pathway through the rooms. This warm light reminds me of God's promise of light. Psalm 119-105 "Thy Word is a lamp unto my feet, and a light unto my path." He says His words will lighten our way in life. Our pilgrimage is guided by God's teachings from the Word. This is a mental picture of God's loving care for us in a time when our surroundings are dark. Every day we see crimes against humanity, decaying morals, dishonesty thriving in business and government and other aspects of life, and we know God makes a lighted path available to those who lose their way. Our Lord is the Shepherd who will lead us if we are willing to follow His directions.

Daily life can wear us down at times, but if we neglect His Word we grow weary and lose our way. God's Word is like a beam of light to our paths.

Psalm Twenty-Three

I memorized the Twenty-Third Psalm many years ago, as most of you, and it's always been special to me. It's one of those beloved chapters that's a favorite of many. The most meaningful thing to me is the first line 'He is My Shepherd." Not just a shepherd or the shepherd, but My Shepherd. That means I am His child, and could not make it without His guidance. Our prayer should be, "Lord, I need you." The Shepherd comes to us in the dark valley of life, for He knows where we are, " for the darkness and light are the same to Him". Psalm 139:11-12.

We call Him Shepherd, but He has many familiar names: Redeemer, Savior, the Light, the Door, the Bread, the Living Water just to name a few, but to me Shepherd fits him best of all. Shepherd is our Savior, our Almighty God, our protector and guide. When we fellowship with Him through the Word we come to know Him in a very personal way – this relationship brings peace that gives us inner contentment. He meets us at dead ends and crossroads, and when we are tired, He comes to us to supply our needs. Books have been written about this Psalm. I read this statement: "When you pray the Twenty-Third Psalm you have prayed every aspect of your faith."

God's Quiet Voice

In one of Charles Stanley's books he states, "Storms are not just inevitable, they are uncontrollable." We cannot control rainstorms, harness floods or tornadoes, for Jesus once told Nicodemus, "The wind blows where it wishes…" When in shelters we worry about our earthly homes, but when storms in life come, remember the foundation on which we stand? Those founded in Jesus Christ can sing, "My hope is built on nothing else than Jesus Christ and His righteousness".

This reminds me of Elijah, a man of ministry in spite of his personal conflict and strife. He was mighty in ministry, but his body grew so weary he wanted to die so he ran to Mount Horeb (Mt. Sinai). I Kings 19 tells us He was near collapse, and no one knew where he was. But God knew and came to him in the cave. God always knows where we are. Like Elijah, we might think we're hidden, but God knows our location. Elijah did not hear God's voice in the wind, or in the earthquakes and fires, but in the quietness of his cave Elijah heard God's still, small voice. We may not hear Him either in the rush of life, but in our quiet time with Him in Bible study He speaks just as He spoke to Elijah. Invest daily moments in His word; you will hear and understand. "Be still and know that I am God. Psalm 46:10

Lover of My Soul

Peace came to my forgiven soul.
He cleansed my past, provided me
everlasting love with joy that last.
He comforts my troubled times,
and in sorrow He dried each tear,
gives strength to me, and tells me
not to fear.

The Shepherd's hands enfold my own;
He lifts me up when I am down,
helps through mistakes I've sown.
All through my life's demands
He sends melodies of grace
from my Blessed Redeemer,
the One, the only Jesus Christ.

Her Words of Wisdom

We never know from what source great words of wisdom may come. I read the story of Malala of Pakistan, the girl shot by the Taliban, who has become a real international inspiration. Her last words spoken to the U.N. were, "They thought the bullets would silence us, but they failed, for out of that silence came thousands of voices." From this statement I realized anew that the silence of a Christian life does speak volumes to the lost world. They see actions of a faithful life and hear words from loving hearts; actions speak louder than words at times. We might ask, "Does my friend, my neighbor or my co-worker witness my faithfulness to the Lord? Will my life have any effect on anyone else? I think of Joshua. God commissioned Joshua to lead the Israelites into the Promised Land. God's challenge was, "Now then, you and all these people get ready to cross the Jordan River into the land I am about to give to the Israelites. (Joshua 1:2) Fear gripped his heart, but God told him to fear not for as I was with Moses, I will be with you."

When we are challenged to speak up, we can know the Lord will speak through us, "As I was with Moses, I will be with you."

Each New Day

God gives us each day, a new start. Someone said recently, "Thank you, Lord, for waking me up today." I say, "Lord, thank you for this day." Either one comes from a grateful heart. I read this morning in Isaiah 32:17, this verse spoke to me. "The fruit of righteousness will be peace; the effect of righteousness will be quietness and confidence forever." Each day holds new beginnings: new friendships, new commitments, and new paths. God knows all about us, forgives, understands, loves and guides us anyway. The reason being He says in Hebrews 10:17 that "He remembers our sins no more." He knows our mistakes, but remains a loving Father. He gives us Grace and speaks peace to our hearts.

Paul calls this the peace "which surpasses all understanding…" in Philippians 4:7. This peace is like a fortress as we arise in peace and calm. Proverbs 20:5 "Counsel in the heart of men is like deep water…" I think of God's peace as a deep pool of quiet, blue water. Years ago when we traveled, we'd sometime camp by rivers of cold, rushing water, other times we'd stop by streams of quiet placid water, deep and blue, a tranquil place to rest. It was as if God had "led us to rest beside these still waters."

Our God Who Sees

This morning I read again Genesis 16 account of Hagar, Sarai's Egyptian handmaiden, who 'ran away from home' fleeing into the wilderness toward her homeland, because Abram's wife made her life unbearable. Hagar stopped from exhaustion near Egypt's border at a desolate spring, where the Angel of the Lord came to her and He knew her name saying, "Hagar, Sarai's handmaid...where are you going?" She told him the story of Sarai's actions toward her after Hagar did what she was told to do. The Angel of the Lord gave her words of hope, for He knew her circumstance of bearing Abram's son, and Sarai becoming jealous and mistreating her. The Angel advised her "to return to your mistress and submit yourself under her hand." Hagar recognized God's presence, calling the Angel, "...the God who sees."

She obeyed and returned to Abram's home on the Angel's advice, then waited for God's plan to unfold. When her son, Ishmael was age thirteen, the Lord completed His long awaited promise. God changed their names to Abraham and Sarah, and their long awaited son was Isaac. A 'miracle baby' in God's time.

Psalms Soft Words

    The Book of Psalms touches every corner of the human soul with its words. We experience a wide range of emotions in life – joy, anger, peacefulness, despair, fear and anxiety, but we don't always share these feelings with others; some so private we hold them close. Some find music and poetry for consolation, and it can all be found in the psalms. The Psalms speak in human words that helps explore and express your feeling to God. King David and other writers of the Psalms had the same feelings and situations that effect our lives today; read of them in their praises, hymns and prayers.

    I love Psalm 19 and Psalm 104 celebrating the creation story. Psalm 23, my favorite for comfort and guidance, with the Shepherd right by my side. Psalm 139 fascinates me, for it tells me so much about myself. In Psalm 13 hear David's plea for God not to forget him. David said, "Lord, I trust in Your unfailing love." There is a psalm for each person and for every emotion and circumstance. The book of Psalms ends with "Let everything that breathes sing praises to the Lord." Praise brings pleasure to God. Our praises to God should be as easy as breathing.

What's Better than Rubies?

Oh, rubies! I love them, but Proverbs 8:11 puts another perspective on them. Solomon says, "Wisdom is better than rubies," and that's not all he says, "All the things that may be desired are not to be compared to wisdom." He tells me godly wisdom is far better than all the rubies of this world. Many today choose money and gold, but God's perspective is eternal, so He tells us wisdom is our most precious asset; it can't be stolen, lost, or decayed, but can be ignored. If we truly want God's wisdom, James 1:5 says "If any of you lacks wisdom, let him ask of God, who gives to all liberally..." God's perspective is of eternal value.

Our best investments are in the lives of others for they go to heaven with us. I quote Billy Graham. "A generation that has sought its own wisdom rather than the wisdom of God is beginning to taste the wine of wrath ..." In Proverbs 3:7 Solomon says, "Do not be wise in your own eyes; fear the Lord and depart from evil." In James 3:17 "The wisdom that is far above rubies is first pure, then peaceable, gentle, willing to yield, full of mercy and good fruits, without partiality and without hypocrisy." The world's wisdom is clever, designing, and conniving, but God-given wisdom is the ruby of life in terms of eternity.

Don't let the Past Haunt You!

Who haunts us with our past? SATAN, he is the great accuser and deceiver; don't listen to him. We have all sinned, but believers can rejoice, because their sins are forgiven forever. David said, in Psalm 103:8-12 "He will not always accuse nor harbor His anger. He does not treat us as our sins deserves...for as high as the heavens are above the earth...as far as the east is from the west, He removed our transgression from us." In Jeremiah 31:34 "...For I forgive their wickedness and will remember their sins no more." Wow, our forgiven past is behind. As God's precious child, never forget this. King David (who had many sins) rebuked Satan with praise. Read the Psalm 18. "I love you, O Lord, my strength. The Lord is my rock, my fortress and my deliverer; in whom I take refuge. He is my shield, the horn of my salvation, my stronghold. I call to the Lord, who is worthy of praise, and I am saved from my enemies..." In everything he praised the Lord.

He is my Shepherd. Psalm 144:2 "He is my loving God...my stronghold, where I take refuge." Focus on praises to Him, then look for victory ahead.

Eyes are Watching You

If a question was asked each Christian, "What do you think your purpose is in this world? The answer should be to reflect the light and love of Christ by your lifestyle. He wants our causal words to honor Him; our actions to show His love. Our insincerity and deceit fools no one. John was a man of gentle love, and he has much to say about love in his writings. One of my favorite is I John 4:7 "Beloved, let us love one another for love is of God..." Someone may ask, "How can I know I love enough?" In I John 5:1 "Whosoever believes (or trusts to the point of believing) is born of God to life everlasting."

His love and respect toward each life you touch will show you are of God. YOU are the only Bible some may read. It's awesome to realize that eyes are upon us in every life situation, and those eyes may be eyes of the lost. We are human mirrors of our Lord, and our reflected images should not be blurred or marred. That image of our Lord can be blurred, by us not clearly communicating the truth.

The heart of the gospel is to live like Jesus. II Timothy 4:4 says the world may turn their ears away from truth, but their eyes capture images they won't be able to forget. Eyes of the lost are watching us, so let us strive to show God's loving nature.

He is Our Shield

He is with us, as our Guide and our Protector. He is a Shield about us. What blessed thoughts are these! This week my attention was turned by an email story about Six Boys and Thirteen Hands. A group visiting the Iwo Jima memorial in Washington, D.C. noticed an older man sitting close by. He was James Bradley, the son of one of the six men raising the flag on that rocky, blood-soaked island during World War II. He said we called them men, but they were 'just boys' ages younger than twenty except one. He named each one and where they came from, as he moved from man to man. Three died and three came home. That big chunk of dark metal came alive to those listening to this man.

God has blessed America, not because we deserve it, but because He has shed His grace on us. The man said, "If you look at this statue closely and count the number of 'hands' raising the flag, there are 13. When the artist who made the statue was asked why 13, he simply said the 13th hand was the hand of God. I had never before heard that nor will I ever forget it. As I read that email I praised God for His mighty faithfulness to our country. Proverbs 30:5 "…He is a shield of those who put their trust in Him."

His Presence

You know why I love the Holy Spirit's presence in me? Ephesians 4:30 says He's the seal of my salvation, the guarantee until the day of redemption that I am God's child. That gives me 'goose bumps.' The Holy Spirit is the bond between me and God. Do we realize that we are led by the person of the Holy Spirit? Each of us is unique and God uses us in our own fashion. He gives each a ministry of God's design, and we should not ever wish to be like someone else, for that's not who God intends you to be.

The Holy Spirit dwells in each believer, and His job is to guide, inspire, comfort, and convict in our daily lives. God has a purpose for each of us, and the more we rely on Him, the more we feel His presence. I equate God's presence in me as a warmth about me. He holds us and gives us inner peace to enrich our lives. The Holy Spirit is a person dwelling in us; He does not impose Himself on us, but waits until He is invited to work in our lives. Paul says in Galatians 5:22-23 the fruits of the Spirit are portrayed in our lives when He is the guiding us, if we resist Him we have negative emotions, judgmental, and an unforgiving spirit. The Holy Spirit wants us to be like Christ.

God Loves us as His Own

The fact that God loves us is not news! God loved us enough to give His Son to die as our Redeemer. Phil Yancey, writes of his doubting experience in his book, Disappointment with God. He went to a cabin in the Colorado mountains to read the Bible for himself and face his doubts about God. From that experience he found God to be real and was amazed to learn how personable He is. He learned Abraham, Moses, David, Isaiah and Jeremiah treated God, as if He was seated in a chair with them. Through his search of the Word he found God to be just that real to him. These articles were of great interest to me because as a young teenager,

God the Father became very real to me, and again I learned first-hand at the loss of my dear husband in 1978, that God loves each of us in His special way. I literally felt His warmth, as He reasoned with me and guided me. He sat with me and comforted me as my memories flowed. I can never again doubt His presence. That experience drew me ever closer to Him for a lifetime. Each believer must spend time with the Lord to really know Him. When we rush through life pushing Him aside, we not only grieve Him, but deny ourselves the fresh, daily renewal from His presence.

Anna

Anna's life story is told in three verses, so why is she even mentioned in the Bible? There has to be something special about this woman that God wants us to realize. Luke speaks of her after Jesus' birth; a prophetess, a female prophet, an inspired messenger who was a pureblood of the Jewish Nation from the Tribe of Asher, one of Jacob's twelve sons. She was eighty-four years old, a widow with no family, so she lived in the temple. She never left for her entire world was in the confines of that building and court yard. I'm sure was an encourager to many.

In Luke 2:36-38, he states that she was living in the temple at Jerusalem when Jesus was born. Luke picks up her story at the visit of Mary and Joseph when Mary's days of purification were complete according to the Law of Moses. At this visit they also encountered a very devout man Simeon from Jerusalem, who blessed Jesus after the Holy Spirit revealed Jesus' true identity to him. Anna talked with Mary and Joseph at that time, and gave "thanks for Jesus and spoke of Him to all those who looked for redemption in Jerusalem." I still wonder why she is in this Bible story, except to show God's faithfulness to her. She lived to see the evidence of the long awaited promise of the Messiah in the child of Jesus Christ.

Benchmarks for a Great Church

The early church in Jerusalem is a picture of a benchmark church. "those who gladly received His words were baptized; and the same day about three thousands souls were added to their number. They devoted themselves to the apostles' teaching and to the fellowship, to the breaking of bread and to prayer." Acts 2:41-42. Many of this great church were personally acquainted with their Savior. It was Christ centered and proclaimed the crucified Christ, resurrected and the indwelling of the Holy Spirit, a praying church, knowing the Lord provides what He approves. It was a church who dared to do things that are only possible with God's help, and existed totally to do God's will.

Our churches today must be the same: a healing church who attend to the hurts of its people both spiritually and physically, a growing church who lifts our Lord Jesus up high to all people, so the lost will be drawn to Him. It prays for its church leaders, guides young Christians, and be a magnetic church that attracts the lost to Christ. It's a joyful church providing spiritual growth, and is committed to spreading the good news gospel. Each member asking, "Lord, what would You have me do?"

I Found Ultimate Security

David said, "In my distress, I called upon the Lord." He found God to be his ultimate protection. Read Psalm 18, its words are comforting for I've had reason to feel like David. God became my true stronghold, my top security. I know Him as God, the Father. These psalms stabilize my thoughts and comforts when my world tilts for some earthly reason. David's concern for life itself, made him fall to his knees for help. Sometimes we face a trauma like uncertainty of job, illness, and other unforeseen things, and appeal to our loving Father.

This was a scary place for David, for he even told his friend, Jonathan in I Samuel 20:3 "There is but a step between me and death." That's how fearful David was for his life. He confessed, "In my distress, I called on the Lord, my God, and He heard me..." God heard him, and David realized he was anchored in the Rock. "The Lord is my Rock, my fortress," He becomes everything to us when we face hard crossings. He can and will lead us to the safe havens of life. Psalm 32:8, "I will instruct you and teach the way you should go. I will counsel you and watch over you." Trust Him in your need.

Learn From David

The devil's kingdom entices us and Satan is a master at setting traps for us, but in spite of this God uses ordinary people to do great things for the Kingdom. David lived, led the people's army, and carried a worshipful attitude in spite of his personal hardships and the nation's woes? He tells us in Psalm 5:7 "My heart is fixed on you, O God, my heart is steadfast and confident." As each year unfolds, we can be secure in God's plan for us. In Matthew 6:33, Jesus told His listeners, "Seek first the Kingdom of God and His righteousness, and all these things will be added to you."

What things? Spiritual things that make us complete with inner security and peace of mind. Any time we face a Goliath, we can do as David did, look not on what we could do, but what God can do through us. As we go through economic battles of unemployment, high prices and hardships, let's say with David. "I can face all this in the Name of the Lord." Put enemies in perspective knowing what God can do. Psalm 16:1 "Keep me safe, O Lord for in You I take refuge." Verse 7 "I will praise the Lord who counsels me, even at night my heart instructs me." God is on our side.

Memorable Time

When I read Joshua 1:1-9 and think back to our early history of Eagle Heights Church. We were a church in the Oklahoma wilderness before we found the seventy-seven acres of land God planned for our church home. That day we joined hands across the land, pressed the soles of our feet on the width of it and walked its length claiming it as our land in the Name of the Lord. As we claimed the land, we claimed the principle of Joshua 1:1-9, God told Joshua "II will give you every place where you set your feet... as I was with Moses, so I will be with you; I will never leave you nor forsake you." He said further, "Be strong and courageous...for the Lord your God will be with you whenever you go." We claimed those promises. This year 2014 we celebrate twenty years, and we have stood strong with God's help through each challenge.

Let us continue to dream king-sized dreams, for God is with us. We are a body of forgiven believers as it says in Ephesians 4:4-6 "There is one body and one Spirit, just as you were called in one hope, one Lord, one faith, one baptism, one God and Father of all, who is above all, through all, and in all of you. So...we go forward in the name of our Lord Jesus Christ.

God's Blue Sky

The sky above seems
to be everywhere,
Its beauty ever ready to appear.
It is always there when
the storm is through,
over the world with a
blanket of blue.
Maybe the sky, wherever
it extends,
and we have no idea
where it ends,
is part of God's lighted
heavenly floor, so
somewhere beyond the blue
there is a door.

Our Constant Refuge

At some point in life you may have felt that everyone and everything had failed you, but you found God right by your side. When our support system weakens, God is there. When we lose loved ones, or any other emotional loss, God is there with His strength. The Lord told Paul in II Corinthians 12:9 "My grace is sufficient for My strength is made perfect in (your) weakness." Paul got the idea, for in verse 10, he said, "For when I am weak, then I am strong." God is faithful. His steadfast love is unchanged.

There is not a place we can go to avoid His presence. Psalm 139:7-12 "Where can I go from Your Spirit? If I ascend to heaven (my life is perfect) You are there. If I make my bed in hell (by my own choices) You are there! If I take the wings of the morning and dwell in the uttermost part of the sea – even there You lead me and Your righteous right hand holds me. Even in the darkness, you are there, for the night and day are the same to you."

We can't escape God and are never out of His sight. I truly thought Grandma had eyes in the back of her head; she always knew what I was doing and where I was. How like God she was in my life. She's been gone since 1977, and I still miss her.

Something Valuable to Know

Being in darkness is not a pleasant place, but I was reminded of darkness when I read about King Cyrus, the king of Persia, who had conquered Babylon while Babylon was holding Israel hostage. God used this Gentile king to free His people. In Isaiah 45:3 God promised King Cyrus "I will give you the treasures of darkness and hidden riches of secret places, so that you may know that I, the Lord who call you by name is the God of Israel." In this case King Cyrus was a deliverer, but I was curious about his treasures of darkness. What treasurers does one find in darkness? The king learned he was dealing with Israel's God, the King of the Universe, and was rewarded with material wealth for releasing God's people.

There are many references about God visiting us during the night's darkness. Psalm 16:7 "I will praise the Lord, who counsels me even at night..." Job asks in 35:10 "Where is God, my Maker, who gives songs in the night." Isaiah 26:9 says "My heart yearns for you at night as in the day." In the night He counsels us, encourages us, and holds us close.

In my own experience when awake at night, the Lord is always there ready to give answers, show the way, or to comfort my troubled heart!

The Lord of History

This title is from Decision Magazine regarding the book of Habakkuk, who faced uncertain economic times as we face today. The Bible shares about individuals and nations, who faced similar hard times, and reveals how God was with them all the way to recovery. The great truth of the Habakkuk's story is he was aware of the impending trouble and disaster, and raised his focus to God. We need to read Habakkuk 3:17 "Though the fig tree does not bud…no grapes on vines…olive crops fail…fields produce no food…no sheep in pens, no cattle in stalls, yet I will rejoice in the Lord. I will be joyful in God, my Savior." What faith he had to make such a statement! He put his trust in the Lord God Almighty who says, "The silver is mine and the gold is mine." Haggi 2:8. The hope in the Lord of history is the same hope we need for our future.

We need a moral and spiritual renewal to face the problems today. " In II Chronicles 7:14 He gives to us the formula, "If My people who are called by my Name will pray and seek My face…humble themselves… turn from their wicked ways, THEN I will hear from heaven and will forgive their sin and heal their land." This should be the prayer for every Christian United States citizen.

My Secret Place

This year on George Washington's birthday I heard some incredible stories of our first President. We know our founding fathers were godly men and relied on God to form this nation, and during the war for our freedom, men were on their knees praying. George Washington called the nation to prayer for an entire day.

This reminds me of a short story I read a few years ago that has stayed with me of how God intervenes. He tells us in Matthew 6:7 "When you pray, do not use vain repetitions as the heathen do…" Just talk to God like a loving friend, and do what He asks, just as the woman did in this story. Her husband was coming home later and later from work; she knew he was stopping at a bar on his way home.

She prayed about it and God inspired her to pray as if she was sitting by his side on his drive home. Long story short – soon he was getting home about on time. One day he confessed, "You know, I often stopped at the bar to just unwind, but now I just drive right by that place." She had to smile for God inspired the idea, she tried it and it worked." She obeyed and God was faithful to answer her prayers.

What is Trust?

Trust is simply the firm belief in the integrity of another person. God's word tells us to trust God, but it's so easy to say, "Just trust the Lord." If you are unsure how to trust Him, these words are meaningless. Psalm 71 is a prayer for the aged, and today I am of that group, and I relate to verse 5 "You are my hope, O God, You are my trust from my youth." This psalm writer must also have been brought up in a Christian home; he knew how to observe God's faithfulness, but not everyone grows up in a Christian atmosphere to know how to trust. Hope and trust are synonymous.

Hebrews 6:19 describes hope as an anchor, "This hope we have is an anchor of the soul, both sure and steadfast..." Without this anchor in Christ, we can drift away from His security.

After the death of my husband of 38 years, I was a wandering soul but learned so much from other broken lives. I learned life does not have to stay empty for there is hope and victory beyond immediate heartaches. He never leaves His children in our despair. He becomes an anchor of trust, and gives us hope and rest in Him.

Why do we Pray?

    My first answer is, "Jesus prayed," so I need to pray. He needed the Father, and we need Him too. Jesus worked on the premise that the Son needed the Father – "the Father and Son are One." If Jesus depended on this path of communication so much, we certainly need the same help, so Jesus gave us the Holy Spirit that connects us directly with the Father. He dwells in us. We talk to God, the Father, and He provides the Holy Spirit in us as our Counselor; to strengthen, convict, to teach, and guides us to keep our lives God-centered.
    Too often we are like Peter; going off on our own way to do things our way. After the resurrection Peter went back to his fishing boat, but Jesus came to him and told Peter to "Cast on the other side" John 21:6. When Peter obeyed he recognized His Lord. Romans 12:13 tell us. "Be steadfast in prayer," and "pray without ceasing." Prayer is not just a time and place, but a mighty force in us when we need Him. There are many ways and times to pray: when sad, busy, troubled, or just in quiet fellowship. Talk to God, for He knows your life and your needs.

Your Adversary

An adversary is one who fights against you. Your enemy can blind, deceive and ensnare you. I Peter 5:8 warns "Be sober, be vigilant, because your adversary, the devil walks about like a roaring lion, seeking whom he may devour." The devil delights in keeping us distracted. It makes no difference how much havoc you've had from him, he will never let you alone, so do as James says in 4:7 "Resist the devil and he will flee. He is actually a coward and can't stand God's word. Peter tells us in 5: 9 the same, "Resist him and be steadfast in the faith." Satan's primary aim is to distract from faithfully serving the Lord by destroying your witness.

More than anything he wants to disrupt us in God's work. He is cunning and annoying, and seeks to destroy. Our decisions must be prayerfully and carefully made. Watch for the devil's wiles mixing in your mind, for he shows up in many forms. God can counteract Satan, if we listen from within for God's still small voice. Satan hates scripture. Watch him run! James 4:7 says, "...he will flee..." We know this, so why do we let Satan 'bug' us?

First Thought in the Morning

As each new day dawns, what is your first thought? Do you thank God for the morning and ask for His blessings and directions? Each day is a new beginning, and the Lord wants to bless us with a new start. We can be robbed of our joy by commitments left unfinished, or nursing something unresolved from yesterday. We carry loads that were never intended to be carried, have worries and battles we need not battle alone, so listen in that first moment of each day, He will provide amazing guidance.

The Lord invites us to live daily in His light. "I am the Light of the world. He who follows Me shall not walk in darkness, but have the light of life" John 8:1. He enables us to see ourselves as we are, and have better days. He can help us lay aside demands that rob us of victory.

Each day can be fresh and clean at the starting line as He wipes the slate clean each day. Don't let anything rob you of this joy as the day begins. From here on when your eyes open and your feet touch the floor, praise your loving Father for who He is, be thankful for this day He has given. He is blessed each morning to hear these words coming from His children.

What Does it Take?

What does it take to have a heart of peace? Isaiah 26:3 tells us, "You will keep him in perfect peace, whose mind is stayed on You..." If you desire inner peace there is the answer. We all seek a peaceful heart at rest, and that's what God wants for us, but most of the time we give God so little of our time that we cheat ourselves. The gift of life is an awesome responsibility, and our time is short so we must give our Lord quality time. James 4:14 asks, "For what is your life? It is a vapor, which appears for a little time then vanishes away." When we trust Him for guidance He gives a peaceful mind and restful heart. My all-time favorite is Philippians 4:5-7 "The Lord is near. Don't worry about anything, but in everything...let your requests be made know to God and the peace of God...will guard your heart and mind..." Paraphrased, a priceless prescription for peace. When we allow our hearts to rest before God, He invades our attitudes, our patience, and will help us deal with whatever makes life discontented and stressed. He gives wisdom when we acknowledge our need and ask for His help. His peace surpasses all our understanding and guards our hearts and minds when we pray, "Teach me Your way, O Lord, I will walk in Your Truth." Psalm 86:11.

Soar on Wings

The longing of the Wright Brothers was to rise up and leave the grassy runway. There must be an inner yearning in man to rise above the bonds of earth. It starts young! How many kids have jumped off garage roofs to fulfill this urge, and ended up with broken limbs. The prophet Isaiah realized man's soul has a longing to fly away and soar on wings from all that hampers him. Isaiah 40:31 "...those who hope in the Lord will renew their strength.

They will soar on wings like eagles, they will run and not grow weary; they will walk and not be faint." Complete trust and utter surrender to Him makes us long to "soar on wings like eagles." We are drawn upward, and especially if Jesus is the Bright Morning Star of our lives. We reach up to Him through the darkness of night as the "morning star rises in our hearts" II Peter 1:19.

I remember another time and place in the dark nights of grief when my soul cried out for rest like David in Psalm 55:6. "Oh, that I had the wings of a dove! I would fly away and be at rest..." It's no wonder we look up: He ascended up to heaven; we look up to Him as we pray, and He illumines our way by His indwelling Spirit. We look up yearning that to be our heavenly home someday.

Man in God's Image

The creation fascinates us, because it's more than we can fathom. The Bible just says, "In the beginning..." Science has other theories. When God finished He approved everything, including man, the crown of His creation. God the Father, God the Son, and God the Holy Spirit decided to make a man. God said, "Let US make man in OUR own image..." Genesis 1:26-27. This man, Adam, was different than all other creations that God spoke into existence. God formed him from the dust of the ground and made him a living Soul to live forever—that part of him is in God's image.

Adam was to fellowship with God, for He made him to think, feel, communicate, and discern. When sin entered, mankind became forever marred by sin, but God made a way for us by sending His Son to die and redeem mankind from Satan. "In Adam all die, even so in Christ all shall be made alive". I Corinthians 15:15-22. Through His sacrifice on the cross and the resurrection He made a way for us as His redeemed children. His still small voice guides us through twists and turns of life, for we are designed for Heaven as our home.

Spring Returns

Sometimes our lives get stale during winter months. We may not even realize what's wrong when we get bored and grumpy. Does this sound familiar or am I describing myself. Winter has its beauty, but spring comes and we rejoice! I'm remembering how we often took days trips in the winter just to get out and away from the usual. We loved mountains, so we drove west to the Wichita Mountains, and upon Mt. Scott, which is the highest point in Oklahoma. We viewed God's winter glory all around.

We listened to crunching twigs and rocks under our feet, then we spotted an old dead tree stump, which had been struck by lightning and died years ago. We first saw its stump and laughed, commenting that's about how we feel at times. We looked over inside the stump and there a tiny green sprout looking up at us.

We looked down at new life coming forth from the dry, dead boredom of the cold winter months. New life and healing can come from old scars and deep wounds, reminding me of Isaiah 11:1 "A shoot will come up from the stump of Jesse, from his roots a Branch will bear fruit..." Little seed sprouts are miracles, that's why spring's new life is wonderful to see.

God's Friend

Can you believe the Lord wants us as friends? I feel so close to Him as His child that it's hard for me to relate to Him as a friend. Jesus says in John 15:14, "You are my friend if you do what I ask you." He also said in John 15:15. "No longer do I call you servants, for a servant does not know what his master is doing, but I call you friends, for all that I heard from My Father I have made known to you, so I call you friends." As our Friend He walks with us and communes with us through His word. Proverbs 18:24 gives us the formula for being a friend. "A man who has friends must himself be friendly, but there is a Friend who sticks closer than a brother." Friends know each other well, and when we face decisions we consult with each other, seek encouragement, and when anxious we seek guidance, when wrong we ask forgiveness, and when happy we share. Friends talk daily.

I'm comforted to know that Jesus, my Lord and my Redeemer is also my Friend. This special Friend abides in me to guide and comfort. I'm reminded of an old song that says, O, what peace we often forfeit, all the needless pain we bear, all because we do not carry everything to God in prayer. Truly, we have a Friend in Jesus!

Wounded Pearl

Actually it's not the pearl that's wounded, but the oyster. A grain of sand invades the oyster, and its internal repair system results in a lustrous pearl. There would be no pearl without a wound. I've been reading the book of Job, and God was so sure of Job's faithfulness that He allowed Satan to prove it. Job did not know this, yet he said, "Though He slay me, I will trust Him." Job 13:15. Wisdom is the pearl of great value. Hear his wisdom in Job 27:3-6, "As long as my breath is in me...my lips will not speak wickedness, nor my tongue utter deceit...till I die I will not put away my integrity. I hold fast to my righteousness, and will not let it go..."

With this awesome affirmation Satan lost his bid for Job's soul. Job longed for the old times, but read Job 29:2-6 and understand his heart. Our wounds of brokenness give us a deeper love and understanding for others. When sadness comes we must think like Job 9:4 "God is wise in heart and mighty in strength..." It seems Job finally understood and said, "He knows the way that I take; when He has tested me, I shall come forth as gold..." Job 23:8-12.

God's Faithful Care

Today I know God cares for me.
I sense His abiding love, and feel
His presence within.

When my needs are great, I reach
up to the Lord above, and feel a surge
of hope, for His grace is always there.
Each day I know God care for me.

I hear His still small voice within—
I quietly listen to hear His guidance
amid my unknown paths.

There He
leads me by the hand in places I
do not know or understand.
It's then
He reveals to me my place of service
in His great master plan.

Four Anchors

Each time I read of Paul's shipwreck adventure in Acts 27, I realize something new about Paul's story. This time I noticed four anchors that were thrown overboard. On their way his two Roman guards transferred Paul to another ship going to Italy, where they ran into serious wind storms. Paul tried to warm them, but no one listens to a prisoner. He reassured them that they were safe, because he knew the Lord was taking him to Rome. His story is very visual and exciting in Acts 27:29 "fearing we would run aground on the rocks, they dropped four anchors from the stern…" Paul was confident in the crisis, for he held onto some special anchors of his own. His anchor of faith that God would get him to Rome. His trust in the Lord's help in any crisis, His hope, for he knew God would see him through this crisis, and Paul's fourth anchor was purpose, he knew God was not through with him, for he was to stand before Caesar. Hebrews 6:19 tells us "This hope we have as an anchor of the soul is sure and steadfast…" Paul's anchors held soundly through his voyage.

We also have shipwrecks in life, and get dashed against the rocks by brutal winds of time. Our Lord provides ports of haven because of anchors set firmly in God's promises.

Red Light Patience

We hear the phrase, "I waited." Most often we hear, "I waited and I waited!" Psalm 40:1 "I waited patiently for the Lord and He inclined to me and heard my cry." Waiting is not one of our favorite things to do, but Psalm 37:7 tells us to "Rest in the Lord, and wait patiently for Him..." We should be pros at waiting, for we wait at the doctor's office, phone calls, guests to come, test results, and red lights. We even wait nine months for our child's birth. I remember waiting on the corner for the streetcar, back when not everyone had a car.

I also remember waiting at the downtown terminal for a transfer. There I watched faces, which created in me an interest in portrait painting. Fretting about waiting is borrowing trouble and worries that may not exist. Satan delights in these frustrations, so he helps us throw our little hissy-fits at being delayed. If we used this time to quiet the spirit and commune with God in these down times how blessed that could be. Better yet, use it as a listening time to the Holy Spirit's wisdom. The Word tells us to wait, this must mean, be calm in spirit.

God never intended for waiting to cause impatience, but for quiet moments to commune with the Him.

Whose Plan?

We talk often of God's plan for each of us, but I don't remember when I first realized that God had a plan for my life. I thought I was choosing my own path, then I read Jeremiah 29:11. "He has a future and hope for us." Psalm 139:16 also tells us He has our days planned and are all written in His book, even before birth, so we are under construction in our lifetime for our special place in His work. I never see one of my daughter's beautiful handmade quilts that I don't marvel at the pattern and her skill and patience. She cuts and fits into an intricate pattern with thousands of stitches. A quilt in progress looks like a jumbled mess, but following the plan it becomes a masterpiece of beauty. I see our own lives being fashioned by the hand of the Master. It's a long process of our wills and God's will conflicting at times, but God never quits working to accomplish His goal.

When my daughter puts on the final binding around the quilt it is finished. God must smile as He watches our lives come to completion during our passing years. One day at His final touch on my life, I will stand before Him as Mary according to His plan for my life."

A Line in the Sand

The saying, "Guard your thoughts and actions as you guard your wallet," brought to mind some incidents while growing up in my grandparents' home. Grandma had her own way of reminding me I'd gotten on the wrong side of the line of conduct. One of Grandma's warnings, "Go on out to play, but don't get dirty!" I never understood her logic, for red dirt was all around me. Safeguarding our minds is to do what Paul warned us in II Corinthians 10:4-5, "bringing every thought into captivity in the obedience of Christ."

Belonging to Christ is a mindset in keeping thoughts and actions in focus, which helps us stay obedient to our Lord. Satan likes to confuse us into believing right is wrong and wrong is okay. Lives today are stained by "red dirt sin," and it becomes okay, because 'everyone does it that way'. Mature Christians are even accepting immoral things as normal, which in the past were 'red dirt sin" in anybody's book.

In our Christian walk a 'line is drawn in the sand,' one side is right and the other is wrong. God warn us, but Satan constantly blurs the line. God's children are in this world, but not of this world. White is white, and black is black!

Sin's Gulf – Love's Bridge

In Eden's Garden selfishness triumphed, and sin robbed the world of love and life as God had intended for us. Sin polluted and separated us from our Holy God, and left its mark of sin on all humanity, but when Jesus came into the world, He brought love back with Him. He showed love in living and how to love each other. His death in all its gory details is a picture of love. When Jesus hung on the cross He triumphed over all sin, death and hell. In Him is all our hope. In our world today love shows tissue-thin compared to the holocaust of crime committed on people, especially on children. Selfish sin is rampant and probably what we hear is just the tip of the iceberg. When I read of how Jesus cried over Jerusalem, just think how He must mourn today as he looks over the world He left, but when He left us at the cross He gave us a bridge over sin's great gulf.

Each of us who have found our way must point the way across the bridge to others to find salvation's love. The Word tells us in Matthew 9:36 "When He saw the people He was moved with compassion for them. They were weary and scattered like sheep without a shepherd." The harvest is white today, we must see it as Jesus sees it.

Furnace of Affliction

In Isaiah 48:10 God told His people, Israel what He was doing, "Behold, I have refined you, but not as silver; I've tested you in the furnace of affliction." This was done because of their unfaithfulness. This happens in massive fires in woodlands when everything lies in charred ruins. Yet tree roots are not effected and seeds lying dormant under leaves and shrubs suddenly burst forth to new growth. God hoped His judgment would draw His people back to Him, for He knew His seeds of love were there to come forth again.

On a recent visit to Arkansas, we saw many old barns that had served well in their day, but now stood in shambles. Yet we saw some restored and Isaiah 53:18-19 came to mind, "Do not remember the former things...See I am doing a new thing..." I could almost hear the old barns groaning under the blows of the hammer going through the 'fire of the restoration,' but now, they stand straight and strong ready for faithful service again.

Don't ever let your life lie in ruins after some 'life affliction,' let God restore you to full service, as David said in Psalm 40:8, "I delight to do Your will." He restores us to become useful as the brand new restored red barns.

Hear the Silence

Our world today is polluted with noises of all kind from road sounds to piped-in music. We've almost lost the ability to be still and know quietness. Psalm 65:7 tells us that God is the one who can "still the noise of the seas and the tumult of the peoples." As God's people we must be still to hear Him. Read Psalm 62:1 "Truly my soul silently waits for God…" I like to listen to the silence of the night in the quiet comfort of home.

When my three grandchildren were small, we often walked on a country road picking up rocks and with nature all around. I said, "Let's stop a minute and just listen." There was not a sound close by. My little brown-eyed granddaughter eased over to me with a questioning fear to whisper she didn't hear anything.

They had never heard silence, so I told them to listen again for birds in the distance. Their faces brightened to the far away sounds. I explained that this is God's world without people noises. He told us to "Be still and know that I am God." Psalm 46:10. Today those three grandchildren are children of the King, and hear God's voice in the beauty of silence.

This Day is all We Have

This is a true statement, today is all we have. Daily we pray, "Give us this day…" Matthew 6:11. This day reminds us that yesterday is gone and tomorrow is not yet here, so what will we do with this day? We cannot survive on yesterdays or tomorrows, so each morning we must praise and thank Him for the day. I thank Him for the many days He has given to me and for all His provisions, even security and comforts that money can't buy. I can't buy breath, a mind to think, memory that holds my treasures, my functioning body, my peace of mind, my salvation or my contented heart.

Without God I have none of these. Nothing – nil- zilch! I breathed in and said "Bless the Lord, O my soul" and breathed out, "All that is within me, bless His holy name." Think about it! If you are fifty years old, He has already given you 18,250 days and each day you've enjoyed the precious gift of life. What we do with our days is up to us. God can direct our daily work as the Holy Spirit prompts us in our willing attitudes.

Each day pray Psalm 5:8, "Lord, make Your way straight before my face." God can make each new day special.

Heart Treasure

The Word warns us about our treasures. Jesus said, "...where your treasure is, there your heart will be also". Christ in our hearts is our true number one treasure, and that treasure can be enjoyed here on earth as well as in heaven later. Since our bodies are treasure chests of the Holy Spirit, He leads us to invest in the lives of others, for those are things we can take to heaven with us. There is nothing wrong with accumulated earthly treasurers, if they don't change our heart's focus from the Lord.

God blesses many Christians with material wealth, while many of us enjoy collecting earthly treasures of various kinds; it happens I've loved jewelry since a little girl stringing and restringing my treasured beads and wearing little dime store rings. I still love jewelry. The point is we can fill our lives with those things we enjoy, so long as we don't let them distract us from the Lord, our real treasure.

Jesus warned people of His day and today about unwise investments that "moths destroys, rust can eat away, and thieves steal." Our souls are eternal, so don't invest in anything that distracts your love and faithfulness for the Lord. Some may be poor in earthly goods, but be the richest people in the state.

God's Picture

We pray to our mental image of God, the Father and it's a joy to Him when we praise with a thankful heart. However, often times we rush in with our wants without first greeting Him. Matthew 6 records the model prayer opening praise as Jesus himself gave it to the disciples, "Our Father in heaven, hallowed be Your name..." Tell Him how you feel such as, Father, You are the God of the universe, Your faithfulness is without end, You are eternal and unchangeable, and we praise Your holy Name.

He desires our thanksgiving and our quiet fellowship. Each morning thank Him for the day He has given. Matthew 6:6 tells us further, "When you pray, go into your room and shut the door, and pray to your Father in secret and your Father who sees in secret will reward you openly." This means quiet time alone with Him. Prayer and reading the Word are primary weapons against Satan, so guard your time spent with the Lord.

Jesus set our example. He often went to the mountains to pray alone with the Father. Paul says "Pray without ceasing," but that does not take the place of praying and reading the Word alone with God. Each time you see His face in your mind's eye, praise Him for who He is.

More than Taste

Salt was scarce and a valuable trade commodity when Jesus lived. Salt was even paid as wages, so the disciples understood what Jesus meant in Matthew 5:13 when He said, "You are the salt of the earth…" Today salt is so common and inexpensive that it's hard for us to grasp the fullness of that statement. We know salt as seasoning and a preservative.

I still remember the smell of meat hanging in Grandpa's smokehouse. Salt was everywhere. God's children has the same preservative effect in the world today. To some degree believers are like restraints on sinfulness; a sanitizing effect, and salty enough to draw thirsty people to Jesus, the Water of life.

Colossians 4:6 tells us that our communication should always be kind and savory, "Let your speech always be with grace, seasoned salt that you may know how you ought to answer each one." The world silently watches to see if we are who we say we are. Jesus calls us the "salt of the earth," a preserving element, and "You are the light of the world," a revealing element in the world. We are a purifier in the midst of sin, a light in the world's darkness.

Four Magic Words

"Peace be with you," are the words, a greeting to His disciples. The words were a jolt to their hearts, because He had died; they had heard He had arisen, but just could not comprehend it. They sat together in the Upper Room when Jesus appeared and spoke these words to them. Each time He met them this was His greeting. He spoke peace to them. Do you believe that He speaks peace to us? Personal peace is a gift of God, for He left it with us. In John 14:27 He said, "Peace I leave with you. My peace I give to you..." It can't be any plainer than that.

Peace or unrest dominates each life, but why are we not at rest since the Holy Spirit dwells in us? Oh, if we could just grasp the comforting power of the Holy Spirit in us. There are many elements which rob us of our joy and peace of mind: memories of personal failure, fears of daily life in general and our selfish attitudes of greed.

Our Lord can change these factors. He forgives failures, He gives power to overcome fear, and He can remove forms of greed holding us hostage. Peace is an open door of faith and we can walk right in to triumphant living.

Old Age

Who wants to think of old age? I sure don't, but I do believe it has sneaked up on my backside. One day I realized that I'm now the oldest living member of my family; I don't see that myself, but I do feel the awesome responsibility standing in the shoes of a strong Christian heritage of God to pass on to my family now. I stand in awe at the path that lies before me. In Isaiah 46"4 "Even to your old age, I am He and even to your gray hairs I will carry you and will deliver you."

I believe God tells us in our old age when losses are great, we will never lose God's loving care. We lose strength, and lose family members and friends in death, and lose even our own health. Some even lose independence and self-worth, but God's love never wavers. Even "I will carry you," He promises. Godly relatives have much to share about God's faithfulness. Their experiences of His caring love and living hardships with God's help are wise counsel to family members.

As a young housewife and mother I often stopped to visit a little neighbor who lived alone. She always made tea which I never cared to drink, but the wisdom that flowed through that dear woman was invaluable to me. She was a wise woman who shared life stories with me.

Heavenly Radar

I recently read how ships navigated the ocean by taking a "celestial fix" on stars to keep their course, today more sophisticated means of navigation are used. There is no better way each day than asking the Lord to show you the way across the unknowns of the day. Psalm 25:4-5. Let this be a daily prayer. "Show me Your ways, O Lord; teach me Your paths. Lead me in Your truth and teach me, for You are the God of my salvation and on You I wait all the day." When we figuratively place our hand in His hand, it keeps us from drifting off the path.

I write so much about the importance of a quiet time; I learned years ago as a child, when I didn't even understand about God, but knew someone guided and comforted me. I lived with my godly grandparents because of my broken home and often sought out places to myself, which Grandma called my 'pouting corners.' One day I climbed an old plum tree in the orchard, and there I found a solace I didn't understand; it seemed 'someone' listened to me. I was drawn back time and time again. It was not until I was about fourteen years old when I accepted Christ as my Savior did I realize who my 'Someone' was who sat in the tree with me. I had learned early to take His hand each day and listen.

More Precious than Gold

What would you say is more precious than gold? Most say life itself, family, and health. Then again, plenty of gold can fix most problems. I Peter 1:7 tells us, "...the genuineness of your faith, being much more precious than gold that perishes, though it is tested by fire, may be found to praise and glory at the revelation of Jesus Christ." Problems test our faith and bring glory to Jesus when He is revealed through our lives. We learn that problems are proving grounds for our faith. Bad times come to all, just as refining polish must come to precious stones. Bad events are often blessings in disguise.

Helen Steiner Rice, the infamous poet who wrote such comfort in her poetry knew personal losses of family, financial insecurity, loneliness, depression, and loss of dependence by a degenerative disease, but through it all she prayed, "Lord, make me a channel of blessing." Her written words came from a wounded soul. Her faith came forth as gold in poetry which comforted, encouraged, and blessed while bringing glory to the name of Jesus Christ.

God's Way

Life's raging storms often press
us hard against the grain,
Making a smooth steady course
each day hard to maintain.

Satan strives to dash our dreams,
and wreck our goals with strife,
leaves us shattered all along
the rugged shores of life.

But we can be assured to find
our way in the wind, for God is
our mighty lighthouse on whom
 we can depend.

Lead m – Guide me

"You are my rock and my fortress; therefore, for Your name's sake; lead me and guide me." Psalm 31:3 Do you ever feel your spiritual well is dry, even while you stand on the Rock in a riverbed of blessings? Each day He gives us a fresh flow of His strength like an artesian power. We take whatever this day holds for us, as we step through His open door of service. A few years ago I found myself on my way to an operating room to repair a broken hip. I thought, "Lord, I know this was not Your plan for me today and it's sure not my plan." When I went away into never-never land I was not afraid for I knew in whose hands I rested. His abiding presence was real to me.

In these 'bumps" in life, He gives courage when we are weak. God's limitless storehouse opens wide to the faithful heart who finds joy in sitting at His feet. Commit a quiet time each day, and don't miss its real purpose, He pours His power and strength in us to handle the pressures of life and refills us when our human resources run thin. Someone said to me one day, "You are so lucky to heal so quickly." I said, "No, I'm not lucky at all. I fell and broke my hip, but I am blessed.

We Pray -We Wait

I like this anonymous quote: "Sometimes the Lord calms the storm, sometime He lets the storm rage and calms the child." God holds us secure when our futures twists in His hands. If we believe nothing passes through our lives but what God allows, then we must know that it has a purpose. Let's do what Job did; he didn't understand through all his pain and loss, but kept trusting God. We pray. We wait. Satan attacks us just because he can, but God s plan goes on, for God is sovereign, and Satan can only stall us temporarily.

All God asks is our faithfulness to continue building His kingdom in spite of Satan's antics. Remember in Acts 1:4 "...He commanded them not to depart...but wait for the Promise from the Father..." Why did Peter and the apostles wait in the upper room after Jesus ascended to heaven? They didn't know they waited for the Promise of the Holy Spirit, our 'Guide' and 'Comforter.'

They just faithfully waited, preaching, teaching and bringing souls into the kingdom. In faithful uncertainty they just 'rested in God's peace."

God has it all under control, though we might not think so, but we trust in God's ultimate plan. We pray – we wait.

I Am With You

These four little words, "I am with you" are the most comforting words to me in the Bible. Some days are harder for there are always worries of rising prices, money matters, worldwide concerns, hangnails, etc. The other day I was bogged down in some real and imaginary problems, and opened the Bible to Haggai and my eyes fell on some underlined words in chapter 1:13, words that God had given Haggai to deliver to His people. Tell them "I am with you."

These words moved them into action, and to some individuals in 2:4 He called on them to "be strong and work, for I am with you, declares the Lord Almighty." Why do we fret when we have such a promise?

Grandpa often said worry is just a mole-hill, so don't make it a mountain. Psalm 37:7 "Rest in the Lord and wait patiently for Him. Do not fret." Lloyd John Ogilvie writes, "Fretting is the misuse of the gift to picture the worst that could happen," when Jesus says, "I am with you," we can be positive of our daily lives. We can walk as Enoch walked in ungodly conditions, yet chose to live righteously. Hebrews 11:5 tells us "God was with him" as He is with us now.

Hope is the Answer

I've been reading Billy Graham's "Hope for the Troubled Heart. " Finding God in the midst of pain is the theme, and he concludes that HOPE is the greatest need for times of trouble and despair. He also says, "Hope, like faith is medicinal to us, but a good part of the world lives without hope." Paul wrote to the Ephesians that they, the Romans were without HOPE, such as many in our world today. The non-Christian world has no HOPE, for they don't know of the heavenly HOPE. In Colossians 1:1-5 Paul tells the church there that they are "saints", not that they were perfect, but that they were Christ-like.

He told them and commended them that "he had heard of their faith, and to him that was evidence of their HOPE, because you have heard and believed from the word of the HOPE which is laid up for you in heaven."

The Christian HOPE of heaven is our goal. God does not need today's high-tech navigation; He has His own global positioning system. He tracks and guides His own by the Holy Spirit. He leads us, yet there are some who do not even attempt to follow His leadership, and without Him there is little contentment.

Roll Away the Darkness

We each go through periods of darkness, but because we are God's children, His light shines as we walk with Him. Paul tells us in Ephesians 5:8, "For you were once darkness, but now you are light in the Lord. Live as children of light." As we walk through personal hurts and tears, it's interesting how others can make us feel closer to God.

In early childhood growing up, Grandpa was my only father-image, I'd sit close to him feeling secure; he was not a big man, but when he'd cup my hands in his I was in ultimate peace. I recognize now that I have felt God's presence through him long before I was aware of God. Grandpa remained an essence of God to me for as long as he lived. I learned caring love from grandparents, for they truly walked as children of light in bad times of our state's history. It was God's love shining through them that rolled away much of the darkness for me.

God's word in times of need is always there for us. Psalm 94: 19 "In the multitude of my anxieties within me, Your comforts delight my soul." I've since learned from living, that God often delivers His greatest blessings during the bleakest times of one's life.

Stay Focused

I'd say we have to "stay focused" on whatever we're doing, but staying spiritually focused should center our lives. When I feel closest to the Lord, is when I talk to Him all the time in my mind. Psalm 63 this morning made me think that David did the same thing. He woke up talking to the Lord: "0 God, You are my God. Early will I seek You. My soul thirsts for You. My flesh longs for You...my lips praise You when I remember You on my bed, I meditate on You in the night watches my soul follows close behind You, Your right hand upholds me..."

Our minds come and go on the Lord during the day and even in the "night watches." I'm reminded of the song, "Always on My Mind. " I don't remember its words nor the artist who made it popular, but the title says what I'm trying to convey. The Lord wants to always be on our minds as we work and play each day. Jeremiah 9:23-24 says "He delights in this kind of living."

My prayer each morning is, "Lord, think Your thoughts through me, so my thoughts will not be scattered and broken, but flow smoothly through me like a river."

A Rainbow Memory

God communicates and we hear His still, small voice amid life's chaos. His eternal promise is in each bow of color in Genesis 9:13-16 spoken to Noah, "I set My rainbow in the cloud, and it shall be the sign of the covenant between Me and the earth. It shall be, when I bring a cloud over the earth, that the rainbow shall be seen, I will remember My covenant...My everlasting covenant." I'd always heard there is a pot of gold at the end of the rainbow, and have wondered how this saying ever came about? Maybe the rainbow is so special, that its end must be priceless. This is my rainbow experience.

Soon after the death of my husband in the late 1970's, I drove through a summer rainstorm to visit family. Being heart broken, I drove through the rain with tears, and when the sun emerged its radiant rainbow colors shimmered intensely against an embankment on my left.

I had never seen a rainbow actually touch the ground. I could have walked into its colors, being on a two-lane highway I pulled to the side and stopped. Whether I saw a phenomenon or God just blessed me with a show of His splendor, I'm grateful every time I remember the rainbow experience.

What Better Fortress

David knew where to run when he needed shelter. In Psalms 17:8 he prayed," ...hide me under the shadow of Your wings." He knew to pray for shelter when he failed or others rose up against him. He was driven to his knees and always found God waiting with strength and guidance. We will find the same also.

This reminds me of Grandma's big Rhode Island Red hens of bronzy-red feathers with her chicks. When the slightest dangers came she'd squat to the ground and her chicks would disappear under her. A perfect picture of God's sheltering love. Every time I read of David's reference to God as his refuge and fortress I remember Psalm 91:1-2 "He who dwells in the secret place of the Most High shall abide under the shadow of the Almighty...He is my refuge and my fortress."

In God's presence we can find a quiet place near His heart, and He wants us to find that place. His shadow falls over us like a shady oasis. We can be refreshed spiritually in any storm of life. I Peter 1:8 says, "...though now you do not see Him, yet believing, you rejoice with joy unspeakable..." the One who calmed the water for the disciples will also speak peace to our troubled hearts.

Crown Him

Jesus says in Matthew 6:33 "...first seek the Kingdom of God and His righteousness..." As Christians we know to do this, but most of us live in a whirlwind of family and busy days of work, school, church, extra activities, friends, and social obligations. God should be our priority, but how can we give Him priority? How can we crown Him each day?

Face the mirror first in the morning to say, "Lord, thank You for this day to live for Your glory." Crown Him each morning of your life. Micah, the prophet asked, "How can I please Jehovah? 'He has shown you, 0 man, what is good, and what the Lord requires of you, but to do justly, to love mercy, and to walk humbly with your God." Deuteronomy 10:12-13 "...what does the Lord your God require of you, but to fear the Lord, to walk in His ways, love and serve Him...and keep His commandments...

This we should do during the day, while we work, shop, attend school, or whatever we do. None of these requirements have gone out of style, and this can be done by crowning Jesus as King every day of our lives.

Security Plus

'My heart is fixed, O God. My heart is steadfast and confident! I will sing and make melody." Psalm 57:7. Bless David! He shows us how it's done. Regardless of what happened, he sang and praised God. Even in the danger of battle, being pursued, family problems, or his own sin and weakness, he had perfect security. David found refuge in the shadow of His wings until calamities and destructive storms passed. He felt God's sheltering wings. We have the same security. David trusted completely, he sang "I will sing and make melody."' We can do the same.

Once the disciples found themselves in a swirling storm at sea, and Jesus came to them walking on the water, John 6:19. We can say like David, "O Lord, my God, in You do I put my trust." Psalm 7:1. Then the Disciples faced a tremendous loss at His death on the cross; they were left astray asking, where do we go from here?

We've all felt this way when loved one is gone, job lost, weakened health, or other hard times? We think all is lost! We forget too, like the disciples had forgotten Jesus' words, until shouts of "He is risen!" Even today we still proclaim, "Hallelujah! Christ is risen!"

I am a Branch

Do you know of the vine and branch relationship? Jesus told us, "I am the Vine, you are the branches" John 15:5. I once planted grapes along my fence. By trial and error I learned to care and prune them to the parent plant each year. I fed and watered them, and they produced grapes galore. I also noted the branches growing directly from the mother plant were the largest, sweetest fruit; this was a perfect picture to me of the Vine and His branches.

If we stay close to our Source by prayer and reading His Word, we grow strong and sturdy. In Genesis 49:22, Jacob refers to his favorite son, Joseph, as "a fruitful bough." Boughs are branches closest to the trunk. That's a description of Joseph's life. His father's description of him as a fruitful branch came about in God's time in His great plan.

The psalmist never heard of the vine and the branch relationship as told by our Lord, but he shared in Psalms 1:3, "He shall be like a tree planted by the rivers of water bringing its fruit forth in season, whose leaf also does not wither..."

Somehow he realized the closer he lived to the heart of God, the more blessed and productive he was.

Special Verbs

In Colossians 2:6-7 Paul gives us some special verbs to live by, "As you have received Christ Jesus the Lord, so walk in Him, rooted and built-up in Him, established in the faith, as you have been taught, abounding in it with thanksgiving." He tells us that we possess faith, so we must practice using it. We are believers and our grand purpose is to glorify the Lord and lead others to Him.

We do this by loving God, obeying, praising, and serving Him. I once heard a song that asked, "if we are the church, why aren't our feet walking, and our hearts reaching out? These three verbs, growing, going, and showing Him to others are the marks of a devoted life in Christ.

I long to be the person God created me to be. We may encounter dark, hard places in life and we all do at times; Isaiah 45:3 calls these times treasures. "I will give you the treasures of darkness…"

These times are hard and leave our hearts wounded and tender, but draws us closer to Him. Moving onward, we grow inward, and showing Him to others is our purpose in life.

The Little Sparrows

Many of us worry each day with so many unknowns: cost of living, crime, mental issues, gun violence, hunger, broken homes, and unemployment to name a few. We worry because it touches all of us. As I sit here today I'm listening to the chatter of busy, little sparrows in a thick Jasmine vines on the back fence. They don't have a care in the world on this cold and windy day. This made me recall what Jesus had to say about them in Luke 12:6-7 "Are not fives sparrows sold for two cents, yet not one of them is forgotten by God...you are of more value than many sparrows."

Even the very poorest of the poor afforded them to sacrifice as worship. Psalm 84:2-3 "My soul yearns for the courts of the Lord; even the sparrow has found a nest for herself." Little birds nested under the eaves of the Temple.

How comforting it is that God chose the lowly, little sparrow to show us this incredible picture of His all-encompassing love. We can't be too insignificant to escapes God's all-seeing-eye. We are worthy because He loves His creation. This kind of love is almost beyond our comprehension, and so blessed that He loves us so much.

Links in a Chain

This morning I read II Peter 1, where Peter teaches the process of spiritual growth after placing our faith in Jesus Christ. "Grace and peace be multiplied to you in the knowledge of God and of Jesus our Lord, as He has given to us all things that pertain to life and godliness, through knowledge of Him ..." He goes on to say in verse 5-8, "..for this very reason, giving all diligence, add to your faith virtue, to virtue knowledge, to knowledge self-control, to self-control perseverance to perseverance godliness, to godliness brotherly kindness, and to brotherly kindness love...for if these things are yours...you will neither be barren and unfruitful in the knowledge of Jesus Christ." This progression builds spiritual character as links of a chain. We are as strong as our weakest link, so we should identify ourselves in this chain. Peter says in verse 10, "for if you do these things YOU will never stumble." Obedience will not allow our weakest link to fail us. II Corinthians 4:6, "The God who commands light to shine out of darkness has shown in our hearts to give the light of knowledge..." We are reflectors of His light and through obedience we strive to not ever be identified as the weakest link.

Ordinary People

The Book of Judges tells us of this period of years after the great leaders of Moses and Joshua. The tribes divided and time passed, there arose a generation who did not even know about the mercies of God toward Israel. These leaderless years resulted in rebellion against God. Judges 3:7 "So the children of Israel did evil in the sight of the Lord. They forgot the Lord their God and served the Baals and Asherachs." God was so angry with them that He let the king of Mesopotamia rule over them until they finally cried out in desperation to Him. His solution was to appoint judges to help return Israel to Him.

His first appointment was an unknown man named Othniel. Judges 3:9-10 "...the Lord raised up a deliverer for them. He chose Othniel, Caleb's nephew..." Whatever Othniel did to help Israel, God let the land rest for forty years until his death, and as before the people reverted right back to their sinful ways without a leader, so God kept appointing judges to keep His people focused on Him.

Othniel was just an ordinary man who chose to do a big job when God ask him. God takes ordinary people like us to accomplish extraordinary things through them.

My Jeweled Path

Look up high onto the mountains
feel warm blue skies this special day.
Seek directions through daily prayer
His bright jewels will light your way.

Set your foot upon the mountain,
your thoughts will rise to heights above,
then once again you'll see this world
as a home filled with joyful love.

Don't look back at your darkest days,
or saddest times of recent past,
just seek God's jewels set before you,
you'll find your treasured peace at last.

The Stable Rock

There are times in life when something happens that makes us search for sure-footing. Our lives are built on the truth of the solid rock promise of Jesus Christ, "...the gates of hell shall not prevail against it." Matthew 16:18. No matter how mighty the winds or stormy waves, our lives will stand, because the gates of hell cannot stop it.

Remember the Lord's conversation with the disciples in Matthew 16. He asked them, "Who do men say that I, the Son of Man, am?" They answered: some say John the Baptist, Jeremiah, or one of the other prophets. Then He looked directly at them, "But who do you say that I am?" Peter blurted, "You are the Christ, the Son of the Living God!"

Jesus declared, "Blessed are you, Simon Bar-Jonah, for flesh and blood has not revealed this to you, but My Father who is in heaven." Verse 18 " on this rock (truth) I will build My church and the gates of Hell shall not prevail against it." Satan knows this Truth, but he never quits trying to stop the Lord's work. He delights in destroying our witness, so we must be faithful for we stand on a solid Rock Foundation of God's promises.

Pray Pray Pray

Find a quiet place in the center core of your being, and there you will find God. Psalm 104:3 "May my meditation be sweet to Him." We all have concerns, so meditate on Him, our loving Father, and let Him talk with you. In those sacred moments He will fill you with perfect peace all though your present circumstances when He reigns in your life.

God told His people in Isaiah 30:15 "In returning to Me and resting in Me, you shall be saved...quietness and a trusting confidence shall be your strength..." When we come to Him with a humble spirit, He replaces our profound restlessness with an inner calm assurance in our souls, which relaxes us in His everlasting arms. With God in control, the indwelling Spirit strengthens and reassures us.

The Lord intervenes and frees us from acute anxieties, which open the floodgates of our hearts and minds to put complete trust in Him. He performs miracles in the lives of people and their problems. So pray for yourself and others. Let's bend our knees and open our hearts, for there are many broken, needy hearts. Let's stay attuned to God's plan and go to those who need us.

All Eyes Forward

"Our God, will you not judge them? For we have no power against this great multitude that is coming against us; nor do we know what to do, but our eyes are upon YOU." II Chronicles 20:12 Jehoshaphat, king of Judah, was threatened with war. The enemy was besieging the land, and they were out-numbered and under equipped. He could have recruited more men, gotten more weapons, but was wise enough to know there was only one real source of help. King Jehoshaphat sought the Lord. The nation of Judah gathered themselves together to ask the Lord for help.

They set all eyes on God, and God spoke through Jahaziel, a Levite in their midst. He spoke God's message to them, "Do not be afraid...for the battle is not yours, but God's." And when you read the rest of the story in that chapter, they believed, they obeyed, and the victory was theirs.

The direction of our eyes is important. When we are besieged by an enemy we turn "our eyes upon the Lord," This battle is not ours, but the Lord's. Our hearts may be broken, but God controls the battlefields and He has plans for each of us to come out the winner.

Unspoken Words

I cannot be a silent witness. Actions of my life speak more loudly than words. Paul wrote in Philippians 1:27 sitting in Roman prison, "Let your conduct (life style) be worthy of the gospel of Christ..." Each day's actions reveal our devotion and love for the Lord. Our allegiance to Him is declared in our attitudes and actions.

I think of Fannie Crosby, though blind, she wrote over seven thousand hymns in her lifetime, which we still sing today. She witnessed in the silence of the writer's pen. Today, we still sing her loving words about the Savior. Remember these? "Rescue the Perishing," "Redeemed by the Blood of the Lamb," "I am 'Thine, O Lord." This person in her blindness blessed the lives of millions. Her words came from an inner God-given reservoir of talent, activated in her by the living Redeemer.

This should make us take a look at ourselves and pray, "Lord, help us put our talents in service for Your glory." We don't have to be center-stage, just let God work His wondrous plan through your own personality.

Rainbow Love

I sat on the patio watching reflections dance on the floor from a small crystal ball dangling in the sun. The movement from the wind, turned the ball as prisms of refracted light made dazzling rainbow colors. Genesis 9: 13-17 "I set My 1rainbow in the cloud, and it shall be a sign of the covenant between Me and the earth when the rainbow is seen in the cloud, I will remember My covenant between Me and you and every living creature..." All I can say is Wow! God's everlasting promise to mankind...just a simple bow across the sky. The actions of His children, show prisms of light, an aura about us which says to the world, "I am God's child."

Look at the rainbow colors: see orange for sunset's restful glow, yellow's sunshine gold, green's still waters, a tinge of red for His saving power, purple-royalty for our King, and blue from Heaven's door. The spectrum of His love reflects in these colors. Ezekiel tells in 1:28 of seeing rainbow colors in the clouds, with a brightness appearing around it as the glory of the Lord, and in Revelation 10:1 John saw a rainbow around the Mighty Angel. We rejoice in each reflected rainbow showing God's beauty.

Happy in Spite of . . .

Today I read Psalm 4, an evening prayer of David's. He must have treaded some deep emotional waters for he said in verse one, "You have relieved me in my distress." Verse seven is the verse that really caught my eye, "You have put gladness in my heart, more than in the seasons when grain and wine increase." That was God's inner peace that gave him comfort and not the bumper crops. Today we have so much, yet discontentment reigns in our lives! Our culture is based on having the best, and more of it. Those who do not know Christ as their Savior never quit seeking more riches, prestige, attention, more and more, because riches and 'things' do not satisfy. The rich young ruler who came to Jesus seeking more; he had much wealth but walked away sorrowfully, because he would not exchange any of it for salvation. That does not mean you can't have wealth and have Jesus too. It's a matter of priority.

Some who walk with the Lord, have learned that the wealth of "things" does not bring happiness. Riches can't come first. James 1:21 tells us to "...lay aside all filthiness and overflow of wickedness..." Many Christians have been blessed with great wealth, and know happiness does not hinge on dollars, but putting God first in their lives.

Hollyhock Seed

One summer I planted hollyhock seeds, those old-fashioned flowers in every yard years ago. They were my favorites in Grandma's yard. I waited and waited for my seed to come up, but was disappointed. Next year there they were and I was blessed with a harvest of blossoms up and down the stalks. This morning I read in Hosea 10:12 where Hosea still had hope for his people, so he told them to "sow to yourselves in righteousness…Break up your fallow ground and plant good seeds, and God will respond by giving you a harvest of love."

When I read this I was reminded to never quit sowing good seeds of God's love in the lives of others. God honors good seeds, but only seeds planted in faith can the Lord bring to harvest. We may not always be around to enjoy the harvest, others may water and nurture, but Galatians 6:9 tells us, "Let us not become weary…for at the proper time, we will reap a harvest." Paul tells us in I Corinthians 3:6-9,"I have planted, Apollos watered, but God gave the increase." God is the Gardener, so we must be faithful to plant.

Prayer Instructions

Prayer is conversation with God; it's fellowship with Him, a communion where He speaks to us through our thoughts. We share with God, our Creator as we pray, and that's where Jesus wants to meet us. He gave us the model of prayer in Matthew 6. We are to call God, our Father, our loving Father in heaven, where His name is hallowed as divine and holy in His place where He extends open arms of Grace to us. Your kingdom come... this to surrender to Him, a statement of commitment, Your will be done. Give us this day means we are dependent on Him for everything - a daily portion. Each day we come as empty vessels. Forgive us our trespasses...

He forgives so our lives will be channels. We cry out, Lead us not into temptation... He would not lead us anywhere except away from evil. Deliver us from evil that's rooted in Satan, and though we are "sealed" in Christ, temptation can overtake us unless we rely on the Lord's strength. For Yours is the Kingdom and power and the glory forever. These are words of submission to God through the blood of Jesus Christ. Amen So be it!

Stress Alarm!

I hope you use Philippians 4:6 and 7 as your stress blocker. "The Lord is near. Don't worry about anything, but in prayer and thanksgiving let your requests be made known to God, and the peace of God , which surpasses all understanding will guard your heart and mind." These words may not be exact, but this is the way I memorized it long ago. There is not a day passes that some part of this verse does not come to my mind. Worry exhausts the mind, depresses the spirit, and damages the body. Stress kills! God gives us the remedy to do what we cannot.

This promise I enjoy reading over and over. "...the peace of God, which surpasses all understanding will guard your heart and mind." The world searches for a quiet peace of mind. Paul tells us in II Corinthians 5:7, "Walk by faith, not by sight." The basis for most of our problems is that we make decisions on what we see or feel, rather than trusting faith. We often fret over our 'borrowed troubles,' when we could praise Him, give thanks and wait for His help. He helps solve real problems and leads us to live victoriously. His peace guards our hearts and minds, so why do we worry?

Special Vessel Just as I Am

At my conception God knew me! He planned my days before I was born. He knows my thoughts. He is acquainted with my ways. He even knows what I am going to say. Read Psalm 139. You have to marvel at what this psalm tells us about God's interest in each individual. I never tire of reading it. I marvel every day at verse 16, "Your eyes saw my substance, being yet unformed. And in Your book they all were written, the days fashioned for me, when as yet there were none of them."

Now, does that not say He fashioned me to be exactly who I am? He knew who I would become, decisions I'd make regarding His Son. Each time I fully comprehend this, my mind is filled with wonder, as to why God made me the individual I am. What special gift did He equip me to do? What number of years are designed for me? Where do I fit in His grand plan? I want to ask God, "How am I doing? Am I fulfilling Your plan for me?"

I cherish who I am in this life, which He gave me many years ago. If we could fully grasp the foreknowledge of God, maybe we could enjoy more fully just who we are.

Building Memories

What brings to your mind special memories of the past: old snapshots, persons, vacations, maybe rocks carried home from the mountains? All these trigger memories of where you've been. I'm a rock collector, and every time I see them in my yard, I remember – the Rockies, the Crystal River, the Oregon Trail, or some special lake or event. These are lasting memories.

This is what God had in mind when He gave Joshua specific directions in Joshua 4 when God told Joshua to have twelve men, one from each tribe, to pick up a stone on his shoulder from the midst of the Jordan River and place where the priests' feet stand firm on the other side. Verse 6 "This will be a sign among you when your children ask in time to come saying, what do these stones mean to you?" These stones were to be a memorial to the children of Israel forever and when children ask, tell them how you crossed over for our mighty God dried up the waters. This rock monument was a tangible memory for their children.

I pray during your lifetime you will keep tokens of memory, maybe not rocks, but good memories to keep forever as a reminder of God's goodness to your family.

God, the Artist

When I read familiar verses that speak to me, I wonder why, since I've read them many times before? God's Word is alive, and it talks to us in our need. This morning Psalms 84 blessed my heart, and filled me with His warm Presence, as I drank deeply of His love. In this psalm David cries out in his joy for God. It seemed David felt like a pilgrim on a long journey and yearned to be at the tabernacle with homefolks. Verse 2, "My soul longs, yes, even faints for the courts of the Lord; my heart and my flesh cry out for the living God."

After being so blessed by this psalm, I opened the patio doors and everywhere I looked I saw the artistry of God. In that moment, I sensed a touch of His presence; His loving care and hope filled my soul. Just a few weeks ago, everything sat barren in the cold, but today flowers are resurrected from the earthen floor with new buds of life, birds chirped louder, as grass turned green. God is at work bringing new life to nature.

Like David, we are on the same pilgrimage to God's Heavenly home, though at times we pass through some parched valleys of life. He closed the psalm with "Blessed is the man who trusts in You!

I Am Here.

The last sentence of Matthews's gospel is, "...lo, I am with you always even to the end of the age." A little phrase, but a powerful message. This is the promise to God's children. An email I received today reminded me of those words. In the email "a man asked to hear God, and a meadow lark sang. He asked God to touch him and a butterfly lit on his hand. He asked to see a miracle and a newborn baby was placed in his arms." The Lord is always near, and we fail to recognize Him.

This brought to mind a childhood memory while living with my grandparents. I crossed a river every day through third grade. It was about half way between school and homes, and for me was a scary place. From the bridge I could see the school and coming home I knew home was near. I'd rush over the bridge and many time I'd see Grandpa standing at the top of the hill waving to me. I look back on this now, and realize how like God Grandpa's silhouette was at the top of the hill. It was God's way of saying, "I am here."

David often said in the psalms, "God is with me," I know He's been with me along my long life. I did not always recognized His nearness, but I knew He was there for "My God, in Him I will trust." Psalm 91:2.

Time Well Spent-

...Emptiness,
    Discouragement,
        Loneliness,
            Distraction,
                Fearfulness,
                    Weakness,
all dilemmas we try to sidestep. God has an antidote for each of these.

For emptiness is "Come, follow Me." discouragement is "Be of good cheer." loneliness is "I will not leave you." distraction is "Be not deceived." fearfulness is "Be not afraid." and weakness is "I am strong." He knows the way to restful pastures, and the Twenty-third Psalm is the path. His Word draws us to Him. He anoints us from life's bruises. He shows us the way each day, as His goodness and mercy surrounds us.

Too often we come to Him half-hearted; usually rushed and don't wait for Him. We hurry on our way, running past the still waters and green pastures, wading through the day's valley on our own without His rod and staff. It's all there, the fellowship and guidance, but we often don't have the time for Him. Stop and feel His touch each day.

In God We Trust

"He who dwells in the secret place of the Most High shall abide under the shadow of the Almighty. I will say of the Lord, He is my refuge and my fortress. My God—in Him will I trust." Psalm 91-1-2. 'In God We Trust' was spoken by the psalmist many years before it became our National Motto in 1956, and on our coins in 1864.

Today this motto is being challenged. I pray our nation will always remain under the influence of the Almighty? Do we live like God is our shelter, our protector and provider? Do we know how to rest in His shadow? This reminds me of an early childhood memory of walking across a wide cotton field in the scorching sun with my Grandpa and asking about the cool shade of a summer cloud that came over us. He said, "Maybe that's God's shadow giving us a cool shade." When I read "abiding under the shadow of the Almighty, I'm reminded of Grandpa's analogy.

During the war in Iraq we saw media pictures of our soldiers being baptized in tanks of water, and that blessed me, for though they trusted powerful weapons, they also realized their need of the Living God. God is our Refuge and our Fortress, and may America never forget that foundational truth, "In God We Trust."

One Way Journey

We could spend hours each day delving into the
past meditating on grief or joys too sweet to last, but
life is a trail, severe and stern, traversed a single way,
step by step we negotiate our trek day by day.

A one way, narrow trail it is, though often we yearn,
we fall, we begin anew, but that day will never return.
Days are not dead nor will they die, like falling leaves
making a carpet, as autumn flails the tallest trees.

Let days recalled be happy days of joy, not sorrow,
let them be a torch to guide our coming tomorrow,
The past is spent, we can't retrace where we've trod,
today only is ours, the past belongs to God.

Learned Attributes,

As a little girl, Grandma was my disciplinarian, and I remember her famous words, "This is best for you. I thought I was being persecuted, but a few years later when I read Romans 5:3-4 and understood. Paul told the church in Rome, "...and not only that, but we also glory in our tribulations knowing that tribulation produces perseverance and perseverance, character, and character hope."

I was able then to see her wisdom. Her 'best' for me were 'corner sessions' building character. I once read a story of old man who grew hardy, strong trees in his yard, and when he planted a new tree, the paperboy watched him daily pick up his newspaper and 'whack' the new tree up and down its trunk. The carrier asked him why. He said that made the tree stronger to withstand the elements. He didn't give his trees much water either, so they would grow deep roots to the water supply. Psalm 1 tells us "...a godly man thirsting for the Word becomes like a tree planted by the rivers of water..." We've all seen God's masterpieces of beauty in old snarled trees rooted in an embankment of a jagged cliff. To me that's picture of a strong Christian rooted in God's eternal values.

I've said all of this to say Grandma's best for me was also God's best, just as the Word tells us.

Real Storage

"For where your treasure is, there your heart will be also." Matthew 6:21. This is a sobering statement made by Jesus. It challenges us to look for what is dominant in our lives, what treasure controls your time and attention? When I think of treasure I see a chest, a trunk, or a bank vault; our treasures can be many things. We amass 'things' of interest that give us joy, but are all perishable. Speaking from experience, it can all be gone is one swipe of a tornado, as my treasures were gone in a tornado.

That's when I saw my own soul as my real heavenly treasure. We can become so entangled in our earthly treasures that we short-change heavenly investments. Our 'things' can dominate our lives that we fail to make deposits into God's work. Material wealth is not condemned unless it keeps our soul container empty and out of focus. What we store in our soul containers is our treasures for eternity.

My real treasure is my personal relationship with our Lord Jesus Christ, and my earthly investments are made in the lives of others. My most valuable treasure is my own soul, and my other investments are made in others, for that is all I will take with me when I'm heaven-bound.

The Small Stuff

God is at work in the big things and small things of life. The big things are good health, good job, and someone dear coming to know Christ. But, there are also many little things in the routine of our day, daily chores, nagging defeats, mundane details that take our time, even the boredom of tasks, and family obligations. Our wise, old prophet, Jeremiah in 32:19 shows that God is interested in our details. "You are great in counsel and mighty in work, for your eyes are open in all the ways of the sons of men, to give everyone according to his ways and according to the fruit of his doings."

Each spring when I clean out the dead leaves and twigs from flower beds, I find underneath a world of insignificant life growing there. I've read when a forest floor is cleared or burned of years' accumulation of leaves called "duff," all kinds of new life and new plants come forth from the ground. The "duff ' of our lives may be things we enjoy daily, but when we rake away that duff we may find new life of God preparing us for something more in life. Lord, help us react to new paths of things unseen and at times not understandable, for You are at work in our lives.

My Shepherd

    I thank God for the Twenty Third Psalm. I'd like to share a few thought about the first phrase, "The Lord is my Shepherd." My shepherd is Jesus Christ. As one of His sheep, my greatest needs are guidance, provision and care. That's what shepherds do. John 10: 3-4 tells us "...he goes before them, and the sheep follow, for they know his voice." To hear, they must follow closely. With this in mind John also says "...he calls His own sheep by name." What a precious thought is that! Does the Shepherd know MY name? Does he call me 'Mary' or does He calls me by a heavenly name? I've been called a lot of names in my life. I am called Friend, Wife, Neighbor, Sweetheart, Mother, and today I am 'Nanny' to my grandchildren and great-grandchildren. Names are no problem for God. Psalm 147:4 "He counts the stars; He calls them all by name." Regardless of what He calls me, I recognize His voice and I follow My Shepherd.

    Over my long years, I've found MY Shepherd close by walking with me. I read of a little four-year-old girl saying she knew the 23rd Psalm, and when asked to recite it, she said, "The Lord is my Shepherd, and that's all I want." She got her words mixed up, but her message right.

What Road?

There is an old saying, "All roads lead to Rome." In the ancient world that may have been true. Today there are systems of road and highways to anywhere you wish to go, but there is only one road to God through repentance. Jesus said, "I am the way..." John 14:6, and the Bible is the road map. This makes me ask why is it so hard for us to stay on course? We have a map; we have a guide, yet we detour and lose our way. In the book of Ecclesiastes Solomon writes of his frustration as one who had everything but he says in chapter 1:12-14, "I was King over Israel in Jerusalem, and I set my heart to seek and search out by wisdom concerning all that is done under heaven, I have seen all the works done under the sun, and indeed, all is vanity and gasping for the wind." Why was Solomon so frustrated in hopelessness and despair? He finally realized that all the possessions and delights of the world were empty and did not satisfy his starving soul.

He finally concluded in 12:14 "...Fear God and keep His commandment for this is man's all, for God brings every work into judgment, every secret thing, whether good or evil." He learned how to follow the narrow path, live humbly and be content with God's blessings.

Our Creator

I know you've watched a hummingbird and have marveled at its ability. It must be the smallest of God's feathered fowls. I marvel of it visiting my honeysuckle vines. Genesis 1:21 tells. us "God created the great sea creatures, and every living thing that moves...and every winged bird...and God saw that it was good" These tiny birds are amazing to watch with unbelievable speed and endurance. They are beautiful, and have a wild courage in their nature. This small bird in God's creation is beyond my comprehension. Our lives are amazing also as we show great faith. Feeding on God's promises from the Holy Word increasing our faith. Romans 10:17 "...faith comes by hearing and hearing by the word of God." We are a reflection of our Lord. The more we look to Him, the more we become like Him and reflect Him to the lost world.

As I watch hummingbirds, I see God in all His greatness and power. There is no other creature in my world that shows me the beauty and splendor of creation more than the magnificent movement of power and might exhibited by this tiny bird. God must have delighted in watching him when He said, "It is good."

Freedom

I overheard a remark from a very sincere person, "I just want to be free." Did he mean no responsibility, no pressures of any kind? This person must be searching for heaven's bliss, but before we achieve that we must pass through life's daily living. A person who wants to shed all of life's woes is one who lacks peace of mind found only in the Lord. There are things in life, which give negative feelings, but Psalm 55:22 tells us to "Cast your burden on the Lord and He will sustain you..." Daily living can make pressures build, and at this point we must look at our time spent with the Lord. When we neglect these precious quiet moments with Him our frustrations increase. The Lord wants us to love the person He made us to be, so we can love others in return.

Paul tells us in Romans 14:19 "...let us pursue the things which make for peace and the things by which one may edify another." There is no lasting peace without a heart at peace with the Lord. Of course, we may have serious problems, but God is always with us. As a child I was troubled about the weights the old Grandfather Clock, but I learned that the clock must have the stress of tension to make it run. We live on the same principal.

He Planned My Day

I've always admired the late Ruth Bell Graham, wife of Billy Graham. I enjoy her poetry, and have read all her books and published articles. She lived alone much of the time raising their five children, while her husband preached around the world. Her faithfulness as a wife and mother is worthy to be called a faithful servant in this duo of evangelistic ministry. Her short article entitled "Such Beautiful Music," she defined great music as compared to Christianity. Some do well, while others struggle. She wrote of a man who lived in a country where God's music wasn't allowed, so he faithfully practiced his music of Handel's Messiah by moving his fingers silently through the entire score on a table top. Our lives may be like a page of music God planned for us each day. In Psalm 139:13-16 " He tells us we are fearfully and wonderfully made in our mothers' wombs and He sees our days fashioned for us, when as yet there were none of them." I pray, " Oh Lord, what did you plan for me to do today?"

It may take just a whisper, a touch, a gesture of loving outspread arms to help someone, so don't hesitate, and as Ruth says, "Play the score just as it is written by the great Composer."

Trials of our Faith

Why are we plagued by trials? Why do we have some hardships in this life? In 1 Peter1:5-7, explains that God's children have a living hope reserved in heaven, and are kept by the power of God through faith. "In this you greatly rejoice, though now for a little while, if need be, you have been grieved by various trails, that the genuineness of your faith, being much more precious than gold that perishes, though it is tested by fire, may be found to praise, honor, and glory to Jesus Christ." It's the end result of a life, not the process of living that is in focus. Life is a testing ground. This was the real truth Peter wanted the people to understand, and it should be our focus too. We prove ourselves every day by being good employees, good parents, good friends, etc. God's proving ground is life where faith is tested.

While experiencing hurts and trials, we wonder what is going on and can't see them as more precious than gold, yet God says they are. Job says in 23: 10 "He knows the way that I take; when He has tested me, I shall come forth as gold."

I Can Do It Myself

This title sounds like a declaration of a three-year old. There is nothing wrong with independence, for our "Me" generation has made the greatest strides in technical knowledge and accomplishments in making this nation what it is today. This we cannot deny, but in so doing, our population in recent years has lost touch with a vital element - GOD. We are today a nation of divided ethics and personal morals and compromise has caused us to veer off away from the GOD of our founding fathers. It has become the philosophy of the day. Billy Graham has addressed this problem to the nation over and over, He said, "This self-confident generation has produced more alcoholics, dope addicts, criminals, wars, broken homes, assaults, embezzlements, murders, and suicides than any generation that ever lived." That we cannot deny! The truth speaks in the news every day.

There is violence and abuse and unhappiness whirling around us. Fear has caused locked doors, and gated enclosures, for we have less trust in GOD, and more in our "I can do it myself ' attitudes. Our plea today should be Jeremiah's cry in Lamentations 3:40: "Let us search out and examine our ways and turn back to God."

This Can Be a Good Day

Can you picture yourself today living free of anxieties, and enjoying the day as it unfolds? This sounds great, and that's the Lord's vision for us. Pray each day, "Lord, give me a vision of who I am and what I should do today, if I totally trust You." That must have been Paul's daily prayer, because he told Timothy in II Timothy 4:17 that in spite of his life difficulties, "The Lord stood with me and strengthened me." This is a comforting fact that we are not alone. In Psalm 139:7-10, the Psalmist asked these probing questions. "Where can I go from Your Spirit? When can I flee from Your presence? If I ascend into heaven, You are there; if I make my bed, in hell, behold You are there. If I take the wings of the morning, and dwell in the utter most parts of the sea, even there Your hand shall lead me, and You r right hand shall hold me." This tells me that He is there with us through life's good times, and bad.

Our Lord wants us to have bright days. In John 1:36 "He looked up, and saw Jesus walking nearby …" Keep your eyes looking upward, and be mindful of His presence with you; be faithful in your commitment for we need Him.

Love's Fragrance

I've always enjoyed the fragrance of perfume. I can recall my grandmother's smell of lavender. I bought my first tiny cobalt blue bottle of "Evening in Paris" perfume sold in dime stores. There is the story of Jesus visiting his friends: Mary, Martha, and Lazarus. After eating Mary broke a box of spikenard and anointed the feet of Jesus. Someone rebuked Mary for being so wasteful, but Jesus saw the deep significance of her act, and said, "Let her alone. She has kept this for the day of my burial." John 1:7. Mary comprehended the Lord's words concerning His death, and anticipated it to be soon. It was not until Mary broke the container did the sweet fragrance fill the room. We too must be broken of self to have His fragrance in our lives. Paul speaks of perfume in 11 Corinthians 2:1 5 "For we are the sweet fragrance of Christ unto God, among those who are being saved and among those who are perishing." We must spend time with Him for His fragrance to permeate our lives.

Good perfumes are expensive, and our fragrance of God also came at a tremendous price, because it cost the life of His only Son. Ephesians 5:2 "Walk in love, as Christ also has loved us, and given Himself for us, an offering and a sacrifice to God for a sweet smelling aroma."

The Stone Man

Andrew brought Simon, his brother to Jesus, and Jesus said when he looked at him, "You are Simon the son of Jonah. You shall be called Cephas." translated a stone.
That's how Simon came by his name, Peter. John 1:41-42 Jesus looked at Simon and saw a brash, uncouth, rugged fisherman with an impulsive foot-in-mouth personality, as a mighty stone in the rough. He called Peter to Him. From the Bible stories we now see what Jesus saw. Jesus called him to follow, and he became like a shadow. He even stepped out of the boat to walk on water toward Jesus.
He drew his sword when Judas identified Jesus as the Messiah. He cut off the ear of the high priest's servant, and was indignant when officers laid hands on Jesus. He and John followed into the courtyard of the high priest, but there Peter's faith failed him. Satan sifted Peter like wheat just as Jesus said in Luke 22:31-34. Yet, Peter ran first to the empty tomb. Jesus saw all this when He looked at him that first day; He saw a masterpiece in the rough.
Jesus also sees our rough edges, but knows a few turns of the potter's wheel will make us ready to serve and be a faithful follower.

Beautiful Feet

"How beautiful...are the feet of him who brings good news, who proclaims peace, who brings glad tidings...who proclaims salvation..." Isaiah 52:7 We don't think of feet being pretty, but He uses the feet of people to do spectacular things through God's strength. Gideon's story in Judges 6 is a story showing that many Bible heroes had doubts and fears just as we do, but finally trusted God to stand with them in victory. Israel's history tells us they had not followed God's instructions, but adopted Baal worship. The Midianites became their enemies, and the people finally cried out to God.

Then God chose Gideon to go with Him into the fields and destroy their idols which enraged the people. Gideon's father, Joash stepped up encouraging him, and God proved to Gideon, by his testing that He truly was with him. Gideon chose to go into battle, and success came because he surrendered to God's cause. God gives us courage to step out with beautiful feet to bring encouragement to others. His Presence in us is our source of peace. Remember Christ does not just give us peace, He is our peace.

For a Lifetime

Now that I'm older, I can enjoy and understand the message God sent to His people in Isaiah 46:4 "Even to your old age and gray hairs, I am He; I am He who will sustain you. I have made you and I will carry you. I will sustain you and will rescue you." When life stretches out before us like an unwritten manuscript, I can testify now that time seems brief. I like Robert Browning words, "Grow old along with me! The best is yet to be..." God knew the nation of Israel, just as He knew us before our births (Psalms 139), and He's had His eye on us ever since.

His promise of a lifetime. It does not mean life is perfect throughout, but He says, "I will sustain you, and will deliver you." There's no need to worry whether we live to old age; God provides eternal security at any age. When young we soon realize dreams may disappoint and opportunities slip away, but our Father is faithful. "Even to your old age and gray hair," God is faithful. Any age can be beautiful. Wherever you are on the road of life, remember Psalm 144:2 tells you He is your loving God and Fortress, your Hightower, your Deliverer, your Shield in whom you can take refuge.

Language of Love

Words—expressions,
the sharing of our thoughts,
some take wings in the wind to
travel into the hearts
of others, then back to us again.

Some encourage and heal, others
bring a smile or just an approval nod;
words of blessings
are sent to us directly
from the heart of God.

A Fragrant Life

This morning I enjoyed reading in II Corinthians 2:14-16, "Now thanks be to God, who always leads us in triumph in Christ and through us spreads everywhere the fragrance of Knowledge of Him. For we are to God the aroma of Christ among those who are being saved and among those who are perishing. To the one we are the smell of death, to the other, the fragrance of life." God's people in the garden of life scatters each day a fragrance of Christ among unbelievers. As I walk in the yard roses may be blooming, and even if blindfolded I'd know they are there. That's what Paul meant by some having an aroma of life to spread the Lord's fragrance. I pray some will smell the fragrance of Christ through our life testimonies.

I had a memory once while doing an audit, when I referred to some old leather bound ledgers, and every time I opened one I immediately thought of my Grandpa. Those old leather ledgers smelled of Grandpa's sweaty leather harness he lifted from the team of horses where the odor lingered. I pray our lives brings a reminder, a sweet aroma of Christ's love to all those about us.

Great Stabilizer

Sometimes, our moods and dispositions change with the winds, because stress sends our anxious hearts into discouragement. Other times, we soar with spurts of energy and other times we can't see the "end of the row." This is the part of life we'd like to avoid. "An anxious heart weighs a man down - but a kind word cheers him up." Proverbs 12:25. Other times we pray 'Be merciful to me, 0 God, be merciful to me! For my soul trusts in You, and in the shadow of Your wings I will make my refuge, until these calamities have passed by." Psalm 57: 1. It takes complete trust in our loving God's sheltering care to survive some adversities in life. Psalm 91:1 reminds me of a place of security, "He who dwells in the shelter of the Most High, shall abide under the shadow of the Almighty."

These are inspirational words for we all need His sense of security. The good news of Christ and His indwelling power calms His children, with encouraging words from others or from His own holy words. This stabilize us, cheers us, encourages us and strengthens us to become like a great oak tree anchored deeply in faith with roots set in the solid Rock. A happy secure Christian is one of patience to wait when the way is not clear.

Rays of Hope

Morning came . . . I'll never forget our demolished home in Moore after the F-5 tornado in 1999. I walked into what was left of my art studio littered with broken frames, tubes of paint, and brushes all scattered and shredded in the wind. I looked at the "mess," then realized the floor of that room was the roof of the storm shelter where eleven of us had huddled from the brute force of that tornado. Eight inches of concrete saved us from death. As I. surveyed the damage, sunlight reflected from shattered glass on the floor, and I was reminded of John 1:4-5 "Through Him all things were made ... In Him was life, and that life was the Light of men. The light shines in the darkness..."

Those sun rays on broken glass reminded me of broken lives I had worked among in my singles Sunday school class. Lives of shattered dreams look like this room, but our Lord sees a broken life and know it can be changed into something beautiful. He can change darkness by a single light ray of hope. "The Lord is near to those who have a broken heart, and saves such as a contrite spirit." Psalm 34:18. Our home lie in shambles, just as broken lives appear ruined forever, but the Lord's touch mends broken lives just as He can restore homes.

Rest in the Lord

When I'm sending encouraging notes, I often urge them to "Rest in the Lord." What I'm saying is, "Since you are sidelined for some reason, just accept it while the Lord heals and strengthens, or draws you aside to clarify His directions. Two years ago I broke my left hip, and I remembered that I'd advised people to rest in the Lord, so I studied God's word about rest. Matthew 11:28 told me to "Come unto me all who are weary and burdened, I will give you rest." I noticed He didn't say go, but come to me. In reality He is a place of rest. His rest is a promise, a gift to us. He says, "I will give you rest."

Rest in Him is our privilege, not retirement from activity, but rest is to heal, strengthen, or plan with the Lord your next project. Some resting-places, may be a sick bed, but most often rest is when we lift upon eagle's wings above our circumstances. Jesus took His Disciples aside to rest; even Jesus went off to Himself to rest and commune with the Father. Mark 6:31 He said, "Come aside by yourselves to a deserted place and rest awhile." Sometimes we need rest and just be quiet to hear the still small voice.

An Empty Vessel

Jesus made Himself of no reputation, and took upon Him the form of a servant, and was made in the likeness of men." Philippians 2:7. Just think of all Jesus gave up when He emptied Himself of heaven's glory to be born a mortal man. From His humble birth to His death on the cross, He accepted every condition and limitation of humanity, and never once sidestepped obeying the Father. We, too must empty ourselves of all allusions of grandeur, picking and choosing what we think is best for us. Just be willing to be an empty vessel, ready to be filled with each available opportunity.

Just think of the dust Jesus carried on His feet walking everywhere, the sweat of heat and weariness of His physical body. His mental pressure from constant seeking crowds, sneers and rejections! This had to hurt Him. He got hungry and stopped to gather wheat and figs, He sleep in the mountains and found rest with the Father. He must have had nagging thoughts of pain and physical death, for He knew that was on the agenda for that last day. He emptied Himself for us. Can we not be an empty vessel ready to serve for Him?

My Own Worry

We hold so tightly to whatever bothers us, and worry about how to handle it. We hold on to worry like a child clutching his toy. It's mine! It's mine! Just the other day, I worried about a situation, held it tightly, struggled along with it even waking in the night to worry. The next morning during my quiet time, the Holy Spirit with His long finger of love, pointed to Philippians 4:5-6 as if to say "Read" "The Lord is near. Do not worry about anything, but in everything by prayer and supplication with thanksgiving let your requests be made known to God." I knew already what it said, for I had memorized it long ago, but I read it again and again and two things, "The Lord is near," and "Don 't worry about anything." said to me, "I am right here. Why are you worried?" After that lesson I even thanked Him for the problem.

    The Holy Spirit urged me to just read those few verses. I read them and learned again that it's more important to read a verse and have understanding than to quickly skim through four chapters. Hebrews 11:6 tells us "to seek Him diligently." He hears us, but it's far more important for us to hear His voice.

Needed: A Guide

I've said it. "If I knew the way, I'd follow it to the letter." Would we, really? God must not have thought so, for He teaches us in Matthew 6 to pray just, "Give us this day ... " Most of us prefer a detailed road map, but all we really need is one day on our uncharted journey. Each day we walk by faith in the unknown that may be a life changing; yet that choice is ours to follow or go our own way. Psalm 25:4-5 "Show me Your ways, 0 Lord; teach me Your paths. Lead me in Your truth ..." What else could we need when we have a Guide to help, teach, and lead? Yet, we selfishly tread upon rocky paths, and get entangled in our harsh experiences. We get too busy to listen, and get confused by underbrush all around, so we make decisions on our own? We all do this. In Psalm 27:11 David prayed, "Teach me Your way, 0 Lord, and lead me in a smooth path ..." That is a blessing of guidance that is ours.

This reminds me of a quote of Billy Graham's: "Each day we stand at the dividing of two streams; one called "yesterday," and the other "tomorrow. We know every bend and turn of yesterday, but the river of tomorrow runs across the unknown. So don't go it alone, we have the Holy Spirit as our escort and He knows the Way.

Floods and Rising Tides

God had promised the Israelites restoration after their captivity. Through Israel, the prophet, God made it clear that He'd take care of them, His covenant people. They were His people and were precious in His eyes. "...Fear not, for I have redeemed you. I have called you by your name. You are Mine. When you pass through the waters, I will be with you, and through the rivers, they shall not overflow you." Isaiah 43: 1-2. In my daily Bible reading in Isaiah, the above verse spoke to me about floods and rising tides we see today. I never read the above passage that I don't remember as a small child watching a raging river near my Grandpa's farm. The swirling water sucked under anything in its path. Whatever troubles we may be passing through right now, His eyes are upon us and He is in control. He doesn't always send help, but says, "I will be with you." He goes with us through deep waters of long bouts of sickness, sorrow, financial woes, family brokenness, or whatever overtakes us. David prayed "Save me, O God, for the waters have come into my soul." Psalm 69:1.

Just remember too, that whatever comes into our lives, is in God's sight, and He will be with us.

Stewards of What?

A steward is a person entrusted with the management of something that's not his own. Often a steward is not popular, but a steward is faithful. Today stewardship is upper most in my mind, for just recently a middle aged couple I know were made guardians of their two grandchildren, ages eight months and three years old. We are stewards of many things in this life, precious lives are entrusted to us as parents, companies entrust their success into the hands of employees. 1 Corinthians 4:2, Paul shows us our greatest stewardship. "...it is required of stewards that a man be found faithful, proving himself worthy of trust." So as stewards of God our greatest trust is The Gospel of Christ. 1 Thessalonians 2:4 "...we have been approved by God to be entrusted with the gospel not as pleasing men, but God who tests our hearts." His gospel is the greatest news in this world, and we are stewards of spreading that gospel. We are to guard its truth and make it known. Each personal testimony spreads the Gospel. That is our faithful stewardship.

Today God is searches for faithful stewards of all ages, who will speak up for His son, Jesus our Redeemer.

Doing My Part

I've just finished reading the book of Exodus, and each time I read God's instructions for building the wilderness Tabernacle and its furnishings, I'm amazed at the details that were needed, exact dimensions, materials, fabrics, designs, and even touches of gold. God asked the people to offer their precious metals, jewels, yarns, threads, skins, stones, wood, and all else that was needed. He also called for artisans to come forth to do the work, and He blessed them with wisdom and skills; for they made each piece of the portable Tabernacle, even the priests' robes.

The beautiful part of this story is God showing His final approval by making a special appearance. "Then the cloud covered the Tent of the Meeting, and the Glory of the Lord filled the tabernacle." Exodus 40:34. In the story we see it took everyone doing his own part to complete this great project, and God used each willing person. His Kingdom is built by our personalities and talents doing what we do best. We may not fully comprehend our roles, or how important our work is to God, for we cannot conceive of what God is building "No eye has seen, no ear has heard, no mind has conceived what God has prepared for those who love Him." I Corinthians 2:9. Yet we are part of it.

Blessed is the Christian . . .

We know these words in Matthew 5: 1-11 as a part of the Sermon on the Mount, called the Beatitudes. "Blessed are the poor...those who mourn...the meek... those who hunger and thirst...the merciful... pure in heart...the peacemakers...those who are persecuted" Luke 6:20 tells us that these words were spoken directly to the twelve disciples like an ordination sermon, though multitudes crowded to heard Him. The beatitudes are descriptions of Christians. These eight Beatitudes are like eight rungs on a ladder that lead to Christian living in peace and joy.

Subjects like poverty, mourning, hunger, meekness, etc. in our way of thinking bring misery, yet spiritual happiness is what we all seek. I was puzzled of being POOR in spirit. I wanted to say, happy and blessed is the person RICH in spirit, but the blessedness of being POOR in spirit means having utter dependence upon God. Now I can say, how blessed I was for that day so many years ago when I realized how spiritually poverty-stricken I was.

Inner spiritual happiness is what we all seek, and being poor in spirit is the royal road to find it.

Paul Says, I Know, I Know

"For I know in whom I have believed and am persuaded that He is able to keep that which I have committed unto Him against that day." II Timothy 1:12. Paul was certain of his personal relationship with his Lord. He told Timothy in verses 13-14 to "Hold fast ...to the sound words which you have heard from me." When we fully commit to Him we deposit our lives to Him through life's journey. Paul told Timothy in II Timothy 4:7-8 "... I have finished the race, I have kept the faith. Now there is in store for me a crown of righteousness ...awarded me on that day" Paul never doubted.

He told the Corinthian Church that our bodies would not live forever, but don't worry, for as our bodies are dying, our souls inhabited by the Holy Spirit, are being prepared for what God has planned for us in heaven. Ephesians I:13-14, "...having believed, you were marked in Him with a seal, the promised Holy Spirit, who is a deposit guaranteeing our inheritance until the redemption of those who are God's possessions to the praise of His glory." What better guarantee can we ask for? John 10:29 "My Father has given them (believers) to me and no one can snatch them out of His Hand..." So no need to wonder about the end results. We can know!

Angelic Signal

Whether it's the Holy Spirit or His ministering angels, our paths are guided and sometimes blocked. This may not be scriptural, but I truly believe this happens. Has a plan ever been thwarted in making a weighty decision? Maybe, you change your mind, and found that your own inclination would have been a grave mistake. Sometimes our paths are blocked. I believe if we truly seek the Lord's guidance, we will find right directions.

This reminds me of Grandma's story of her grandfather, a Baptist circuit preacher, riding his horse on Saturday to find the meeting place for Sunday meetings in towns and small unknown areas. He might ride into a place in late evening to stay with someone for Sunday services, and on occasion he had trouble finding the right place. One evening he saw a tiny light flicker through the trees that led him to a small cabin; dogs barked; the cabin door opened, as they welcomed the preacher for Sunday's meeting at a small nearby church. He never questioned the light that guided him for he never doubted that he'd be divinely led to the right place, so two young teenage boys could hear the gospel and be saved. Grandma always said, "I believe an angel held the tiny light for Grandpa that night."

Side by Side

Hearing the news one day reminded me of two little trees about three feet tall I once found growing side by side down the lane. Grandpa moved them to the yard for us to watch grow into shade trees. One appeared weaker as they grew side by side with the same care, sunshine and soil. The summer passed, then the smaller tree did not survive the winter. Grandpa cut it down and found that it was infested and destroyed from within. The news today reminded me of the little tree that struggled to live, but died of an infestation. We are watching people grow up side-by-side like my twin trees, but some dying of Satan's infestation. How do we help them? "Lord, show me Your ways..." Psalm 25:4. Only we can show these lost souls the way across the great gulf fixed between them and God. We watch these poor, dying people nationwide, running headlong into so-called glamorous and fun-loving times, and all the while Satan is destroying them.

"Search me, O God, and know my heart, test me and know my anxious thoughts and lead me in the way everlasting." Psalm 139:23-24. We must pray, Lord, help us to somehow reach them, before they waste away in Satan's infested soil, as surely as my little shade tree.

The Calm of Inner Peace

I read Billy Graham's "Peace with God" published in 1953, and now I've read his second revision, and I've been blessed again. He reaffirms his timeless message of how to maintain God's peace. We search for ways to feel close to God. He tells us that too often we associate love with feelings, feelings come and go, but commitment stabilizes our devotion. Look at his guidelines. READ THE BIBLE DAILY: Its spiritual food. Read, study, meditate, and memorize it. LEARN TO PRAY: The Holy Spirit will teach you. Without prayer you will never know God's inner peace. RELY ON THE HOLY SPIRIT: Your body is the dwelling place of the Third Person of the Trinity. Stand aside and let Him help you with your decisions. ATTEND CHURCH REGULARLY: Christianity is a fellowship of believers. The building is only a place to worship. LIVE ABOVE YOUR CIRCUMSTANCES: God made you who you are and placed you where you are to live victoriously in whatever living conditions you abide.

Blessings

My life is blessed in many ways,
happy sounds of laughter whirl around
and sunshine falls upon my floor.
Happy sounds of love with friends
make good times with them.

Fragrant lilacs scents sail around my head
peach blossoms and iris appear.
Flowers grow and spreads along the wall,
birds' happy sounds are heard nearby.

Turtledoves cooing their lifetime love—
warms my heart with love till death
does part. The night's silvery silence
comes to give me rest for each new day.

My life is ever warmed with happiness
day by day, for I am so richly blessed,
from God's love above.

Designer Creator

I watched the History Channel the other day explaining how the world came to be; scientists just can't accept God's Word? "For by Him all things were created that are in heaven and on earth, visible and invisible...all things were created through Him and for Him. He is before all things and in Him all things hold together." Colossians 1:16-17. Human beings are so insignificant in the scheme of things, yet are so loved by God. God is the Supreme Being of all creation of this world. Below God are the Angels, then the Cherubims, guardians of God's holiness (Genesis 3:24). The Seraphims continually worship God for His holiness (Isaiah 6:23), and though we're made in God's image, we are below the angels. When Jesus was born a human being, He became lower than the Angels (Hebrews 2:9).

Then after His death, resurrection and ascension, He returned to His rightful place at the right hand of God, Ephesians 1:20-21. So, in our insignificance, we so loved by God because we are made in His own image to love and worship Him. "For God so loved ..." "See, I have even inscribed you on the psalm of My hand." Isaiah 49:16. No one can explain the world's existence any further than the first four words of Genesis 1: "In the beginning God," but scientists will not accept it.

Power-Packed Words

"Deny self - Take up cross daily - Follow Me" Then Jesus said to them all, "If anyone desires to come after Me, let him DENY HIMSELF, and TAKE US HIS CROSS DAILY, and FOLLOW ME." Luke 9:23. This is called the true cost of discipleship. Taking up your cross daily is a voluntary action of accepting what He wants you to do. You have your cross, I have mine, and He wants this commitment from all of us. Sometimes we let our yearnings to succeed and gain in this world become our greatest desire, and often this blocks the Lord's voice to us. Many have learned that the Lord's way is best and follow Him.

Ernest Hemingway, the well-known writer, was once challenged to write a story in six words. He penned: "Baby shoes for sale. Never worn. " He regarded this as his greatest work. With few words Jesus conveyed His challenge: "deny self, take up cross daily and follow Me." We can deny Him so easily by not speaking when a good opportunity comes our way to tell of Him or praise Him. It may be hard to follow Him at times, but it's been proven to be the best way. How do you score on discipleship?

God's Night Song

"By day the Lord directs His love, at night His song is with me a prayer to the God of my life."
Psalms 42: 8

When I awaken in the morning after a restless night, I read God's Word. I'm usually led to some marked scriptures in my Bible, which have blessed me over and over for years. As I've grown older, these restless nights are more frequent, so the Lord quickens His special words stored in my heart. Just last night I quoted some of David's thoughts in Psalm 42, where David told God about his hard times and depressed feelings, "I pour out my soul within me." David asked, "0 my soul, why are you cast down? Why are you disturbed within me?" Verse Six he made a plea to God, "0 my God, my soul is cast down within me." He said I sit here in deep thought, and You show loving kindness in the daytime and at night a Song to me. Verse nine, "I say to God, my Rock, why must I go mourning, oppressed by my enemies? .David asked himself again, "Why are you cast down, 0 my soul?" He answered his own question, "Yet, I have hope in God and I will praise Him, my Savior, my God." I may not hear a song, but a peaceful comfort surrounds me, as sleep comes at last.

Cover With Love

The color of the Golden Rule is still in style. It's always golden. "Do to others what you would have them do to you." Luke 6:31. The Golden Rule covers mistakes with a coat of love. We all make mistakes, and we expect understanding, instead of the justice we deserve. Jesus made it plain that we are to love friend and foe. This rule must work both ways, and if we practiced this rule, it could change the history. This Golden Rule is more valuable than gold, and is beyond measure between people; if we combined the love in I Corinthians 13 and the Golden Rule we'd have a perfect combination. In summary, love is like light shining through a prism from the lives of Christians living by the fruit of the Spirit: love, joy, peace, patience, kindness, gentleness, humility, and self-control. Galatians 5:22-23. These ingredients not only make our lives happy, but bring love and fairness for others. "We are to forgive as the Lord forgave you, and with all of these virtues put on love, which binds us all together in perfect unity." Colossians 3: 12- 14.

The Golden Rule is God's way of blessing us, so we may bless others.

Magnify Him

Psalm 34:3 "0 Magnify the Lord, and let us exalt His name together." I never hear the word magnify that I don't think of Grandpa's magnifying glass. It was handled almost reverently. I could not touch it, but he'd hold it and let me look. It was like magic to me. We wish to get a more detailed look of God with our natural eyes, but we must see Him through faith. Through human eyes, we see Him high and lifted up, while our spiritual eyes see Him magnified in glory and honor. He is worthy of our highest praise, so we praise His Holy Name. The greatest way to exalt Him is helping others see Him as their saving Redeemer. We honor and exalt Him by our own lifestyles. We must remember that all the wondrous things of this life is but a shadow compared to what He has planned for His children.

Paul says in Philippians 1:20 "...Christ will be magnified in my own body whether by life or by death." Luke 1:46. This tells me that we magnify God by the way we live. Our purpose for living as children of God is to show Him to the lost and dying world around us. II John 1:6 says, "...His command is that we walk in love." Loving Him makes Him increase while we decrease, as John the Baptist did in proclaiming, "Behold, the Lamb of God..." He magnified the Lord Jesus Christ to others around him.

Something Priceless

When we think of things priceless, of course we think of life's breath, salvation, family, comforts, peace, food, and untold opportunities. We probably also think of jewelry and other world commodities unattainable by just ordinary people, but some people do own much worldly wealth. As a child I had a cigar box that held my priceless possessions of arrowheads, glass beads, rings, and special other things. They were valuable to me, because I could not replace them.

The Proverbs speak of God's wisdom, an attribute of God that can actually be one of our rich earthly possessions. "Blessed or happy is the man that finds wisdom, and the man that gains understanding, for wisdom is more profitable than silver, and yields better returns that gold more precious than rubies, nothing you desire can compare with wisdom." Proverbs 3:13-15. The Proverbs describe the weight of wisdom exceeding earthly treasures, it is beyond price. Worldly treasure can vanish, but His treasures have eternal value. According to King Solomon writer of the Proverbs, we need to attain wisdom and discipline for understanding in seeking a disciplined life. Reading the Proverbs daily gives us His wise counsel in small morsels.

Today is Wonderful

The reason I say today is wonderful is because, "This is the day the Lord has made, we will rejoice and be glad in it." Psalm 118.24. God made this day, and He didn't make it to waste or misuse; it is a gift. I pray "May the Lord direct your hearts unto God's love and steadfastness of Christ." II Thessalonians 3:5. When we realize that in Christ we have everything we need, we can rejoice in whatever each day holds for us. I remember the day at age ten when my Mother came for me to live with her. I recall the fear of her house, away from all I'd known at Grandma and Grandpa's house. Each day was strange to me, but soon my young, trusting heart responded to new things and new people. I'd awake each day to something new: my new stepfather, new friends, new school, and new things to see and learn. God blessed this child each day. I know now it was the Lord who took away my fear and replaced it with positive things so I could be happy. I'll never forget, and still praise the Lord for the memory of it, and how He cared for me as I awakened each new day ready to experience what He had planned for me.

Our Personal High Priest

Thinking of Jesus as my High Priest is foreign to me, yet it's true. He gives us divine access to God, the Father, but to me He is my Lord and Savior. Hebrews 4: 14, 16 tells us, "Seeing then that we have a great High Priest who has gone through the heavens, Jesus the Son God, let us hold firmly to the faith we profess ...Let us therefore approach the throne of grace with confidence, so that we may receive mercy and find grace to help us in our time of need." He's our personal Savior who took on flesh and blood to experience all we deal with daily, and then sacrificed His life for us, to become our HIGH PRIEST, yet I see Jesus as my risen Redeemer, and my Shepherd. He meets our needs, though He sits in a place beside God the Father on a throne of Grace. "He gathers the lambs in His arms and carries them close to His heart..." Isaiah 40: 11. I love this scripture for it pictures our Lord's Shepherd heart. Some things are hard to understand for we just see the here and now, and not the scope of God's plan, so we live and wait trusting our Lord. God is real. God loves us. He hears us. His plan unfolds, and we can know that someday, "we will dwell in the house of the Lord forever" with Him.

Good Health Plan

We each have health concerns, and desire to live a long life. A healthy life is nothing new to God, for the Bible talks of this. Proverbs 3:1-7 "...let your heart keep my commands for length of days, and long life and peace will be added to you." Verses 5-7 most of us know by memory: "Trust in the Lord with all your heart, lean not on your own understanding, and He will direct your path. Do not be wise in your own eyes, fear the Lord and depart from evil. It will be health to your flesh, and strength to your bones." The book of Leviticus tells us that God gave Moses detailed instructions on health issues. God taught them how to worship, how to be holy, and serve a holy God. This is still the basis of a healthy, godly life today Many nuggets of truth are scattered throughout scripture on how to have a good life. We have fear and worry that damages the mind and body, but Philippians 4:6-7 is a formula for God's people to live by, and are my all-time favorite. "The Lord is near. Do not worry about anything, but in everything by prayer and thanksgiving, let your request be known to God and the peace of God, which surpasses all understanding, will guard your heart and mind through Jesus Christ, our Lord."

Times and Places

In my walk with the Lord I remember special places where I've vividly sensed God's presence. They are like a cool oasis on a long memory journey. In the 1940's we lived in a town of about of five thousand people, and were members of the First Baptist Church. I'll never forget that building, red brick, gothic in design, like many old churches in small towns today. It had a pipe organ, stained-glass windows, and dark oak wood pews. It seemed God's presence lingered there, for any time you entered, you felt His presence. I remember a time after my husband's death in the seventies, I felt the Lord's warm presence holding me close in a restful place until I could go on. These rich places of memories are where we rest and rejoice, or even hide in Him for a time. Jeremiah 6:16 says, "Ask for the old paths where the way is good, and walk in it, then you will find rest for your souls." It's all right to look back, but not a place to dwell.

The Lord blesses each service as we sing and praise, and hear the Word preached, but the real oasis I'm talking about is the quiet time with Him when His still small voice speaks, and you will feel warmth from His presence.

Foundation in the Darkness

A sure foundation is an unmovable object beneath, like our faith in Christ, a perfect example of having a Rock under our lives. Our world today, much like the world Jesus was born into, is full of uncertainty because of wars and terrorism around the world, crime, earthquakes, shattered homes, and economic problems. Today a majority of the world lives in darkness, because they search for help everywhere except from the true and living God. They look to mankind and government for solutions, instead of a loving God to help them walk in this darkness. Their hearts are empty, even in the affluent society in America; they continue to plunge headlong into the deeper darkness without God's light.

God's love flickers all around them from God's people, but they seem blinded with hopelessness. Jesus came as a baby to "seek and save that which was lost" Luke 19. He later told them to "come to Me, all who labor and are heavy laden, I'll give you rest" Matthew 11:28. Our lights of faith should flicker brightly as we walk with those in this dark world. I remember well the faith of my grandparents showing me how we were securely tucked away in His care.

God's Heart Desire

I've given thought to these words, "I will give them a heart to know Me, that I am the Lord; and they will be My people and I will be their God, for they will return to Me with their whole hearts." Jeremiah 24:7. I love that scripture, for it makes me realize just how much God desires our love and faithfulness. Jeremiah was born to be used of God. When God called him as a youth, this is what He told Jeremiah, "I formed you in the womb. I knew you, and before you were born I sanctified you; I ordained you a prophet to the nations." Those words must have burned in Jeremiah's heart many times during those forty year of abusive torture for delivering God's message of doom and judgment. God's people plunged into Babylonian captivity for seventy years. God so desired they would return to Him with hearts ready to receive Him. He wanted them to love and serve Him, but that did not happen, so God sent His Son to die for all of us. Today He still desires our love and faithfulness with surrendered hearts, for He loves us with an everlasting love and desires our praise and worship. "By this they know that you are my disciples..." John 13:3-35. This is the key to spreading His love.

Don't Hoard God's Blessings

Remember this old hymn written in 1897? Count Your Blessings? Remember these familiar words? "When upon life's billows you are tempest tossed, when you are discouraged, thinking all is lost, count your many blessings, name them one by one, and it will surprise you what the Lord has done. Are you ever burdened with a load of care? Does the cross seem heavy you are called to bear? Count your many blessing, every doubt will fly, and you will be singing as the days go by." The words may not be exact, but I remember this old song, and often count my many blessings, and praise Him for His hand that works in my behalf. His blessings are gifts of peace, contentment, provisions, and He leads in ways we cannot envision. He works behind the scene, and deserves our praise and acknowledgment of His presence. He provides blessings money cannot buy.

It's important for us to share our blessings with others, and be living examples of happiness and joy from our lives. Speak of your blessings, just as you speak of your hurts and your needs. "Count your many blessings, name them one by one, Count your many blessings, and see what God has done."

My View of Me

Do you long to be more than you think you are? James 4:10 tells us to "Humble yourselves in the sight of the Lord, and He will lift you up." If you have questions of how to live and what God expects from you, the book of James is helpful. You are anointed to be the person God called you to be, so don't let anything or anyone steal your uniqueness. Sometimes we create in ourselves an envy or stress to be like someone else. We are each unique by design. What a boring world that would be if He made us all the same. God made each according to His divine plan to serve Him in our way, and speak His words in our own way. You may be the only one to reach a certain person for the Kingdom. I love to listen to beautiful singing voices, but I can't sing well; yet I can praise the Lord because of someone's beautiful voice. Maybe you will read something I write and be blessed. God uses each of us by our own designed fashion.

I know that we are to do what God designed us to do, if we keep busy serving in our places and roles doing what He asks of us. I know when we are faithful, God's work will abound, our souls will be lifted up and blessed, and God will be glorified.

Attic Retreat

Do you remember those places of childhood where you played make believe in shades of old oak trees? You could live anywhere and be anyone you wanted to be. At times, even now, it's good to step back into our retreats, and feel His closeness. In Zephaniah 3:17 it says to me, "The Lord your God is with you... He will take great delight in you, He will quiet you with His love, He will rejoice over you with singing." I have mentioned in my writing several times of Grandma's attic room which I visited regularly, especially on rainy days. It was a dusty, little room with soft light spilling through the one small east window. I'd climb the ladder on the wall and sit among her treasures of old trunks, boxes and cast-offs which she said we might need someday. Old family things intrigued me.

Now I still envision that place tucked safely away in my cache of memories; I close my eyes and see myself there again. I rejoice as I view again life memories. We should tell Him every day, "Lord, You have been my dwelling place...before the mountains were born or You brought forth the earth and world from everlasting to everlasting, You are God." Psalm 90: 1.

Prolific Vine

The Father says "I am the Vine,
you are the branches, if you abide in me."
The Lord's amazing love surges through
my veins, so I bear fruit serving Him.
He cuts off the limbs, which weigh me
down, and pull me back into sin.

He prunes away to multiply
each fruitful branch of life—
glorious new growth
makes branches full
of service and blessings both.

They Came -They Saw

The lowly shepherds of the hills found the Baby, and their great message was tidings of great joy. Today the Christmas story is still joy. It's a joy that Paul call a fruit of the Spirit in Galatians 5:22, "love, joy, and peace." "Joy and hope are anchors of the soul, both sure and steadfast," as we're told in Hebrews 6:19. The precious gift that the Lord gives us every day of the year is, "Lo, I will be with you always." The Shepherds returned to the hills glorifying and praising God for all the things that they had heard and seen, and told to them. Luke 2:20. Their lives were all changed as they returned to their own ways of living. Don't hang on to today's conflicts, for we know our hope is built on God's faithfulness. "He is the Anchor of the soul, both sure and steadfast." Hebrews 16:19. God loves with an everlasting love. This endears God to us for we cannot comprehend that kind of never ending love, a gift from our Lord, "It is I, do not be afraid." This gift is for everyone. The gift is yours. Open it! Treasure it! Trust it! Hold it close! It is gift wrapped in God's faithfulness.

A Refreshed Vision

The changing of leadership in any realm of our lives brings unrest and uncertainty, especially the election of new leadership for our nation. We need God's wisdom in making all our decisions. I'm reminded of Isaiah after King Uzziah died. The king was not only his king, but his dear friend, so Isaiah went to the temple at this crisis in his life. There the Lord revealed Himself to him. "I saw the Lord seated on a throne high and exalted, and the train of His robe filled the temple." In that scene angels were about Him singing, "Holy, holy, holy is the Lord Almighty; the whole earth is full of His glory." Isaiah 6:1. From that experience Isaiah realized anew that God was God, for all majesty and power were displayed for him. This reminded Isaiah that God was still on the throne, and though his friend was gone and the earthly throne had changed, God is eternal, and earthly events do not change God.

Many of us are disturbed about worldly crisis, but we're to seek God's wisdom, and realize that our eternal God is in control and we are to shift our outlook from people, world and national problems to a vision of our Eternal God in control. God under-girds us as we face the future.

The Masks We Wear

Halloween is around the corner, and soon we will have many guests visit our front porch. Who are they? We can't be sure, because they wear masks. Do we sometime wear masks, so that no one really knows us? Often we think we know a person by what we see, but Jesus spoke of the Pharisees in Matthew 15:8, "These people draw near to me with their mouths and honor me with their lips, but their hearts are far from me." Many claim to know God, but are not genuine. They wear masks, and later their actions reveal their inner selves. The Pharisees acted haughtily and spiritually correct, but did not accept the true picture, so they wore masks to cover their contempt for Christ. Jesus knew their hearts. Some today may hide but only fool themselves. Stop and dwell on this! Are we caught up in our own lives so much that we forget to serve Him? We look at each other to see only the outside, but God looks at the heart. This was a very sad statement Jesus quoted about the leaders of His day. They wanted to follow God, but were blinded by their own masks of deceit.

Joy in Life

In Billy Graham's classic book, "The Secret of Happiness," he says after studying through the Beatitudes himself, he realized Christ was giving a formula for personal happiness, regardless of age, or circumstances. After reading the book again after many years, and seeing his explanation, I, too, can see the Lord's character put into words. I highly recommend this book. Many search for happiness, but some never find what they seek. You may be a millionaire, blessed with fame, beauty, and popularity, and still have nothing but a miserable life of loneliness and despondency. The Beatitudes are ancient truths that can result in the peace and happiness we seek daily. Paul's letter in Philippians 4:11 tell them they can have peace in all circumstances. "Not that I speak to need, for I have learned in whatever state I am, to be content." We know of Paul's dire needs at times, yet he was content. Things are not always perfect, yet we can believe and draw closer to Him; He strengthens our faith and blesses us, as we find joy of living in God's peace.

Year-Around-Garden

My favorite old hymn as a child was "In the Garden," because its words brought such wonderment to me of strolling through the garden with God like Grandma did. She'd sing that old hymn in her vegetable garden with colorful flowers and grape vines hanging on the fence.

As a little girl I'd listen. "He walks with me and He talks with me, and He tells me I am His own" I remember peeking through the grapevines to see if I could see Grandma and God walking together. I even searched for His tracks - such a precious memory to me. Its spring now, and I enjoy sitting on the patio or on a bench under the tree thinking of God and my fellowship with Him is real. Not many conditions exist today that we can still enjoy the beauty of creation and His peace in us. We can meet Him any time or anywhere and be refreshed.

Don't wait for a perfect time for your quiet time, just make time and be faithful. Choose to walk in peace and contentment and He will bless you in mind, body, and soul. Your daily relationship with the Lord, will fill you with peace and confidence, as He meets you each time in the rose garden of your heart.

Sanctuary

I don't remember when I came to realize the real meaning of the word sanctuary. The word always made me think of a place of peace and safety. There's very few Bible references that use the word sanctuary. In Leviticus 16:33, the holy sanctuary is described in the priests' duties, but we find the word refuge used often in David's psalms. Refuge translated means a secure dwelling in the rock. Psalm 71:3 David prayed, "Be my strong refuge...You are my rock, my fortress." We've all felt overwhelmed at times when our pasts haunt us, so we daily search for security.

Hear David's heart, "0 God do not be far from me. You are my hope - You are my trust, my strong refuge. (Psalm 31:3) He says, "You are my rock and my fortress. Psalm 91 "He is my refuge and my fortress." David also speaks of "dwelling in the secret place of the Most High - abiding under the shadows of the Almighty." That's the ultimate security and sanctuary. There are many types of safe havens, but our most restful is home abiding under the shelter of His wings. This a blessed sanctuary.

Somewhere today shut out the world and enter into your sanctuary with God. Love Him, praise Him, and hear Him speak. He says, "Be still, and know that I am God."

Gideon's Story

Each year in my daily Bible reading I look forward to the book of Judges to read again of Gideon. I see myself, and the rest of us in this account of the Children of Israel waffling back and forth to God. Over and over God sent someone to their rescue, and this time it was Gideon. The Angel of the Lord said, "The Lord is with you, oh mighty man of valor!" Gideon was shocked. "Lord, who me, a mighty man of valor?" God looks where we cannot see, so read Gideon's story of excuses, much as we often do. Gideon quickly said, "My Lord, how can I save Israel? My clan is the weakest, and I am the least of my father's house."

Gideon finally said, "You show me a sign that it is You who talks with me." Gideon tested God twice with the fleece of wool on the threshing floor. We've all asked for answers like that, so God proved that He was with him, and the story goes on to tell of Gideon's great victories with God's help. Judges 7:21 is a victorious verse, "Every man stood in his place around the camp, and the whole enemy army ran out and fled." God uses ordinary people like you and I to do great things for Him.

A Red Carpet

We've watched people walk the red carpet and heard acceptance speeches with thanks to many, with tears, and incoherent babblings. Recently I read an article of an acceptance speech for a Nobel Peace Prize. The writer said it would have been so perfect if he had just said, "This is an awesome honor, but what is more awesome is the fact that I know God, and He helped me attain this honor." This reminded me of Paul's words in Philippians 3:5-7 where he named his own credits. He said, "I am of the stock of Israel, of the tribe of Benjamin, a Pharisee, a Hebrew of the Hebrews, but what things were gain to me, these I have counted loss for Christ." Paul's desire was "that I may know Him and the power of His resurrection..." Christ was real to him, and Christ's resurrection is also our hope because of our salvation experience. Seen by many after the resurrection proves He is real, and is the greatest miracle of all times.

In Hebrews 11 named those of great faith. You or I will probably never walk a red carpet, but one day we will see the red carpet rolled out before us for of the Lamb. "Our faith is the substance of things hoped for, and the evidence of things not seen." Hebrews 11:1.

Listen in Silent Moments

Silence today is almost non-existent. Sounds of our world are all about us from every conceivable source. Again, I'm remembering my long ago childhood days with my grandparents. Each evening we gathered on the cool back porch, washed-up and rested after "supper" to laugh, and listen to someone's tale of the day. In silent moments we listened to bird sounds far away, owls in oak trees and sounds from the outside. In our busy world today, I often wonder do we actually hear God's still small voice? Psalm 46: 10 "Be still, and know that I am God." We need to listen for God's private whispers to us. I've always believed God wants to speak with us in a two way conversation in prayer. I truly believe drawing apart alone in prayer is the most basic kind of prayer. That's when we can shut out the world and meet with the Father in secret. Group prayers are good, but drawing apart alone with Him is vital at times. When in prayer I can speak privately to the Lord. Being still and quiet, I "feel" His warm presence with me. "The Lord is near to all who call on Him, to all who call on Him in truth." Psalm 145: 18.

Just Words

Have you ever known a person who has an artesian flow of words? In reading God's word, we are warned of our words. In Matthew 5:37 in Jesus' Sermon on the Mount, He urged the people to let your "yes" be yes and your "no" be no. In other words be true to your words. Paul says in Colossians 4:6, "Let your speech always be with grace, seasoned with salt, that you may know how to answer each one." John 7:38 Jesus speaks, "He who believes in me, as the scripture has said, out of his heart will flow rivers of living water." What comes out of our mouths is dependent on what's in our hearts. James 3:6-11, warns about the tongue, which can produce both blessings and curses. Words overflowing from a righteous heart brings joy and peace.

I have a friend of words and laughter. Gales of laughter flow from her mouth as she shares everyday life. In fun she was given her Indian name of "Talks-Alotta." She accepted it with joy. She has a beautiful "Ministry of Laughter" to ladies groups. Her talent spreads God's word in laughter and love. Our words become our testimony.

God is Faithful

In the spring I sit on the patio looking at flowers and shrubs that return each year, and I'm reminded of God's faithfulness. Moses said it so well in Deuteronomy 7:9, "Therefore, know that the Lord your God, He is God, the faithful God, who keeps covenant and mercy for a thousand generations with those who love Him and keep His commandments." This is restated in I Corinthians 1:9 "God is faithful, by whom you were called into the fellowship of His Son, Jesus Christ our Lord." It is food for my soul to walk and pray outside among growing things. This goes far back into my childhood on the farm with my grandparents.

I still remember findings things as a child: wild flowers, a rock or some strange-looking branch. Grandma's yard was also filled with clumps of lavender phlox, lilies and white daisies by the garden fence, lilacs, pink clusters of roses called Seven Sisters, morning glories and honeysuckle vines everywhere, and I can 't forget the hollyhocks leaning against the old, unpainted house. What a delightful place to live and play growing up. Even today, its memories still bless me. The Lord is always with us, and if you look back many of us can almost see the Shepherd's tracks along our way, as I do.

Prayer is Fruitful

To pray daily makes us so attuned with the One who guides us, that His thoughts become our thoughts, His desires our desires, and His nature becomes our nature. Prayer is so helpful that even Jesus needed to pray in Matthew 14:23. Prayer leads to a closer walk to become His voice, His hands and His feet. Praying is just half of the process, for we must listen. Jeremiah 29:12-13 "Then you will call upon Me and go and pray to Me, and I will listen to you. And you will seek Me and find Me, when you search for Me with all your Heart." Paul also tells us in Philippians 4:6 "Let your requests be made known to Him..."

When someone comes to mind, the Holy Spirit is prompting us to pray for that person. We may not know why, we don't need to know - just pray, for God knows. Romans 8:26 "...For we do not know what we should pray for as we ought, but the Spirit Himself makes intercession for us•..." Jesus tells us to pray about everything, and as we pray, to approach Him as "Our Father" Matthew 6.

Prayer develops a relationship of surrender to Him, a closer walk with Him. A quiet testimony is one who walks daily in prayer and depends on God for everything.

Listen to the Father

One of my first thoughts after accepting Christ as my Savior was He will never leave me. I've found this to be a true realization over these many years. He's been a true companion to me. A daily quiet time keeps our fellowship close as He reveals Himself to me. He knows me and is a personal Father. As Creator He tells me in Psalm 139 some special facts about me. He knew me in my mother womb. He formed my body, soul and spirit, and wrote in His book the days fashioned for me when as yet there were none of them. So I take comfort in knowing that I can trust His guidance each day.

Let me paraphrase my thoughts about the Father. He says: I know your needs, your bruises and heartaches. I know your human frailty, just trust Me. I am Truth. I can help you, heal you, restore you and give you peace. I know where you are at all times, and you can be assured that I am always near. I am your Shepherd. We walk together. I'm aware of your inherited traits, your past, your yearnings, and your struggles. Talk to me daily, and you can always know I am your ever-present Father.

Devil Next Door!

I read an article recently by Ann Spangler, "When the Devil Lives Next Door." I immediately thought of a grumpy neighbor, but it was not that, but the fact in this world all around us is the devil's kingdom, and he may just live next door. Satan dwells among us, but we need not panic for our beloved John reminds us in I John 4:4 "...the One who is in you is greater than he who is in the world." That promise is incredible! But, we must stay armed with the weapons of Christ, plus love, humility, and obedience to the Father, fully armed with "the sword of the Spirit, the Word of God." When we worry about the devil's battle with us, just brag on your blessings, and he will flee from you. There is no set time or place to pray. Paul says in Ephesians 2:19, "Through Him we have access by one Spirit to the Father."

As Christians we have the responsibility to live by our faith, have a faithful prayer life and read God's Word. When you figure Satan lives next door, or even in your own home, just remember the Bible is clear that Satan has no power over you, and he will flee from God's words spoken from your mouth.

God's Space

An article in Open Windows devotional book this week made me aware of my body as the temple of God, and how we often violate His space. I Corinthians 3:16 "Do you not know that you are the temple of God, and that the Spirit of God dwells in you?" It is hard to realize fully that there is a definite part of me that is occupied by the Holy Spirit, and it's a sacred place, which we can so easily dishonor by thoughts or a selfish lifestyle. God's space is special, for we gave that part of us to God for occupancy, when we trusted Jesus as our Lord and Savior. God prepared this place for Himself. He tells us in Ephesians 3:17 "...that Christ may dwell in your hearts through faith... rooted and grounded in love..."

Our lifestyles can affect His image to others by our life testimonies. We pray each day for wisdom as Solomon prayed in Kings 3:9 "Therefore give to Your servant understanding and a heart to judge that I may discern between good and evil..." We pray for this wisdom to keep our temples clean and pure. When we give allegiance to things that displace Him, it grieves Him greatly. God's space in me is sacred, and I must be ever aware of His occupancy.

I am Sure

There is no doubt of His gift of salvation,
this He freely gave to me.
I am confident. I am secure.

He lifted me with everlasting love,
now I am anchored in Him,
my vision changed. I am secure.

My faith was tested, my needs were great.
I found His grace sufficient
I know I am loved. I am secure.

His majestic presence is within me.
I am a child of the King,
I am confident. I am secure.

God's Power in our Lives

God in the person of the Holy Spirit is the power in our lives. The Bible is clear that the Holy Spirit is God Himself. Paul's final greetings in II Corinthians 13:14 about the function of each. "May the GRACE of the Lord Jesus Christ, and the LOVE of God, and the FELLOWSHIP of the Holy Spirit be with you all." We don t understand the Trinity, but accept it by faith. II Peter 1:20-21 that, "...no prophecy was ever made by an act of human will, but holy men moved by the Holy Spirit." The Holy Spirit speaks and guides us to live by His will.

The most comforting thing about the Holy Spirit's presence in me is the fact that His seal was set in me the night I accepted Christ as my Savior. In Ephesians 1:13 Paul tells us "...having believed you were marked in Him with a seal, the promised Holy Spirit, who is the deposit guaranteeing our inheritance until the day of redemption..." Paul further warns in 4:30 "And do not grieve the Holy Spirit of God, with whom you were sealed for the day of redemption." The Holy Spirit leads, guides, and teaches us to live in His will. The Holy Spirit does His work through us.

Perfect Timing

Time is a homeward journey. We look at life as time between birth and death. I am convinced it's like Solomon says in Ecclesiastes 3: 1-8, "To everything there is a season, a time for every purpose under heaven...a time to be born and a time to die..." Solomon says that a life not centered in God is purposeless, and without God, nothing can satisfy. This is an honest confession of a man who had everything and lost sight of God. He meant humanity in general, but the truth is if we leave out God, we find nothing but emptiness. Many Americans today have everything, but nothing satisfies. A good man may have a good life (not necessarily free of hard times) but he chooses to live godly. After all the good, bad, and selfish devices of do's and don'ts, Solomon's conclusion is told in the last two verses of the book, "Now all has been heard, here is the conclusion of the matter: Fear God and keep His commandments for this is the whole duty of man. For God will bring every deed into judgment whether it is good or evil."

Just let God's big hand close gently over yours when concerned about life, and you'll feel secure, for He sees your tears, your long stare into the future. He is our loving God who walks every step with you on your journey.

A Mosaic Snapshot

I've often wondered how God will see us at the end of life. His words, "It is finished!" were the words that allowed God to rip the temple veil from top to bottom, which separated us from Him. His resurrection from the grave was the crowning victory, so God has set two ways before us, "the narrow gate and the broad gate, but "...narrow is the gate and difficult is the way which leads to life, and few will find it." Matthew 7:13-14. Some say there are many ways to God, but in truth there is only one way, Jesus says, 4:6. "I am the Way...and no one comes to God, the Father except through me." At my workplace in the lobby hung a beautiful wall-sized painting in mosaic forms of a beach area called Turner Falls. At a glance you knew what it was, though it was just a study of colors. Could our lives be like a series of mosaic snapshots that God sees at a glance? If God is our Savior, our daily lives should give to others a glimpse of Him.

My grandparents have been gone many, many years, but their life and words still help me like snapshots of godly wisdom. I pray my life will be like mosaic pieces of life and words that portray Christ to my family.

Let Your Life be as Sunshine

A remnant is a small piece of something left over, like materials or nuts and bolts from a project. In scripture a remnant is referred to as a small number of people left as a nucleus of God's people. Long before the prophets, God used Noah and his family, and used Joseph in Egypt to save the remnant during a worldwide famine. Moses warned Israel in Deuteronomy 4:27, "The Lord will scatter you among the peoples, and only a few of you will survive..." Isaiah, the prophet proclaimed Israel's doom in Isaiah 1:9, "Unless the Lord Almighty had left us some survivors, we would have become like Sodom and Gomorrah."

The New Testament carries on the same plan, which includes both Jews and Gentiles. Paul explaining to the church in Romans 11:1 5, "I say then, has God cast away His people? Certainly not! I am an Israelite, a seed of Abraham...Even so then, at this present time there is a remnant chosen by grace..." From this history we see God preserves a remnant to serve as a light in the midst of darkness. Today we are the children of Light. That's our challenge today. This "light," passed to us must be carried to those around us. Psalm 139: 12 challenges us, "Let us be good stewards of the Light that is in us."

Inspired Beauty

I took a double-take at the beauty before my eyes one morning in the back yard. I stopped at the sight of it, and remembered the way the yard looked when we moved here after the 1999 storm in Moore had destroyed our home. Our broken lives at that time felt as bare and bleak as this yard looked, but the Lord has not only blessed and restored us, but also the yard. Today I read in Song of Solomon the love poem between the Bridegroom and His bride. It refers to flowering beauties and sweet scents, and that reminds me of how God must love the beauty of sunsets, flowers, the vast universe, even tiny mountain flowers so perfectly made. He loves the beauty of nature, and I see Him as the Lover of our souls, the Rose of Sharon, and the Lily of the valley.

God not only changed our lives but He changed our yard as we planted shrubs and flowers. He's now building for us a City in heaven that Paul tells us in I Corinthians 2:9 "No eye has seen, no ear has heard, no mind has conceived what God has prepared for those who love Him." That boggles my mind, that one day all those washed in the blood of the Lamb will look upon the Bright and Morning Star in God's Garden in Heaven.

"Will Never Cease"

In every changing season I see God's everlasting promise made to Noah. When Noah came out of the ark he built an altar to the Lord, and "The Lord smelled the pleasing aroma and said in His heart, never again will I curse the ground and never again will I destroy all the living creatures, as I have done. As long as the earth endures, seedtime and harvest, cold and heat, summer and winter, day and night will never cease." Genesis 8:21-22. God loves our praise and in this I see His heart of love for His people. As His treasures He loves our faithfulness, and grieves at our neglect of Him, but verse 21 goes on to say, "Never again will I curse the ground because of man, even though every inclination of his heart is evil from childhood." It was after this that He made the universal covenant with Noah, "I establish My covenant with You, between Me and you and every living creature. This is a covenant to all generations to come. I set My rain bow in the cloud as a sign and I will see it and remember the everlasting coven ant between Me and all life on earth." (My paraphrase of Genesis 9:8-17)

Today there are few sure things in this world, but these covenants are real. We may someday destroy or blow ourselves to smithereens, but not by the hand of God.

Our Comfy Ways

I read this quote of evangelist, D.L. Moody: he once approached a stranger on a Chicago street and asked, "Sir, are you a Christian?" The man answered, "Mind your own business!" Moody replied, "Sir, this is my business." This reminds me of the many committed hearts who tell the Gospel Story. Many of us have become so settled in our comfy ways of life, that we've lost our passion to win souls for the Kingdom. We must realize that many people spiritually lost are all around us, and we must become missionaries to our neighbors, co-workers, friends, and family. Let's pray for that missionary heart to abide within each of us. We have gifts and talents that could change the world, if each committed Christian would reach out. Too many of us say I can't, but like Paul in Philippians 1:6, we must "Being confident of this very thing, that He who .has begun a good work in you will complete it until the day of Jesus Christ." God's faithfulness under girds us and empowers us to do whatever He calls us to do. If we simply tell them what God has done in our own lives the Holy Spirit will use our words to draw them to Him. Words of our testimonies can mean life and death to others. Share your own story at every opportunity.

A God-Honored Woman

An honored woman, so well described in Proverbs 31 was a wise woman, and we don't even know her name. So much has been said about this working woman, wife and mother, that she stands tall as an example for women.
Society today bombards us of what is deemed beautiful, but most of it is so shallow. Many women make their lives miserable by empty glamour, but I pray that Christian women will compare themselves by the high standard this woman in Proverbs. "Charm is deceptive, and beauty is fleeting, but a woman who fears the Lord is to be praised." I'm remembering a favorite saying of my Grandmother, when I was a teenage "Pretty is as pretty does," and that was accompanied by a serious discussion of actions, attitudes and values of a person.
The description of this wise woman covers a variety of personal issues in her life. She was not perfect, but was wise in how she conducted her life. The writer of Proverbs complimented her busy, productive life. This book is full of truisms and illustrations that expose some realities of life. She is described as an ideal woman; wise in all areas of her life, a busy woman with "a quiet spirit and precious in God's sight."
I Peter 3:3.

Moments to Remember

With grateful hearts we Americans should be the happiest people on earth, for we are the most blessed, in spite of all the heart breaking "stuff' in our nation today. God's faithfulness continues. I often wonder why and how can God stand us? Recently I was blessed by the news of the memorial for the USS Oklahoma in Hawaii honoring the 429 young souls who died there. This reminded me of the stone markers we read about in the Bible. Joshua 4 (paraphrased) When the whole nation had crossed the Jordan, the Lord told Joshua to choose twelve men, one from each tribe, to take up twelve stones from the middle of the Jordan where the priests stood, and carry them over and put them down at the place where you stay tonight. In the future when your children ask, "What do these stones mean?" Tell them the story of what God did when we crossed the Jordan River.

Our historical memorials markers also show us of God's faithfulness to America. In Oklahoma our godly ancestors are remembered among old Oak trees in cemeteries dotting our state. May each kind of memorial standing transmit God's loving faithfulness to our nation.

Arc of Light

Sometimes in early hours in my quiet world reading God's word, I hear familiar sounds that bless my life with contentment. My thought amazes me that God has given me memory to recall the past, good and bad over my long years. Memory is one of God's most precious gifts; to look back and see God's rainbow of love. The world technology in many ways has marched beyond me; yet in the midst of all this I see unrest, storms, wars, and tragic turmoil around the world. It seems our entire world is in darkness; yet we know His Light shines, for you can't have darkness without light. Rest and comfort in this darkness is real for it comes from our Lord. Our anxieties have increased; Satan's battle rage openly around the world, even natural disasters and economic affairs run rampant. We ask how do unbelievers cope without God's love and light in their hearts? Our Christian witness is vital to those who do not know how to find God's peace. Each witness from us simply tells them of God's inner peace during their life uncertainties.

We can take heart in these dark conditions, for God is an Arc of Light shining over us. Nothing escapes His eyes, for God sees in the darkness, for nothing obstructs His view, for Psalm 139:11-12 tells us "that the dark and light are the same to Him."

Always There

"Behind the dark unknown stands God within the shadows keeping watch over His own."--James Russell Lowell. I'd say with each person there comes a time when that person says," I'm depressed. I've bottomed out." In reading Jeremiah's story, he was at that point when he cried out to God after weeping and preaching to deaf ears for forty years. He told God, "You have moved my soul far from peace...My strength and my hope have perished." Lamentations 3:14:18. He felt he'd been treated badly and God had allowed it, but Jeremiah concluded in verses 20-24 "I recall to my mind...Great is Your faithfulness." He began remembering all that God had done and realized anew God's love never deceases, and His faithfulness never ceases. He said in verses 22-23 "...His compassion fails not...They are new every morning." So, when you get "down" and say, "Woe is me," remember God's love surrounds you anew each day. I've also found it's okay to look back occasionally and remember the past goodness of God is your life. At times I may not see His hand, but in hindsight we see evidence of His guidance. These good memories are good resting places. Just look, and see His hand in your life.

Modern Giants

As I read the daily paper and flip through TV channels, I'm ashamed at what I see and hear. I pray, "God, forgive us for what our children are being exposed. God's morals are no longer "normal." Now in many ways wrong is right, and right is wrong. In fact, right is often ridiculed. Billy Graham says, "The world today is on an immoral binge that has not been known since the days of Rome . . .we see human nature expressing itself without God." Today many live by "what is right in their own eyes." From God's word I learn from Caleb, one of the spies Moses sent to survey the land of Canaan, the promised home for God's people. Numbers 13:14. Some spies returned defeated and afraid for they had seen giant descendants of Anak, while Caleb saw the same giant warriors, but knew God was with His people with unlimited power. When I get discouraged I also see problems like monsters, but the Lord encourages my heart to think like Caleb; see the world yet know God's help is available. We must teach our children to live by God's laws, even if our world is morally bankrupt. We can instill in our children that God is a great and mighty Friend, and they have His help to slay any giant who threatens them, be it drugs, crimes, or whatever. This concept must be taught to our children, but also must be lived before them.

Godly Wisdom

"Wisdom is the principal thing. Therefore get wisdom, and in all your getting, get understanding." Proverbs 4:7. "If any of you lack wisdom, let him ask of God..." James 1:5, and "...knowledge of wisdom is sweet to your soul..." Proverbs 24:14.

Wisdom originates from God. It is not something we acquire quickly, it's a process of learning. We must seek God's wisdom by absorbing His truths, and applying obedience to His principles. We are to ask for wisdom to follow God's guidance, and observe what God is doing in the lives of other Christians, and join them. That is a great principle I learned in the MASTERLIFE study. Join in and be a part of God's agenda. God places godly people in our midst to guide and teach us; just as babies must walk with a hand held firmly until he grows and has enough wisdom to be safe in basic living. We too, must hold fast to God's basics until we have wisdom to walk wisely. God's wisdom is not a mystery or unattainable, for you have wise counsel available, no matter what life challenges you are facing right now. Being "yoked with Christ" is a lifetime commitment, and wisdom comes from His word, and walking faithfully in a relationship with God, the Father; you are strengthened by His Spirit. Ephesians 3:14-21.

God Does Not Chitchat

"God does not chitchat" is a quote from the Charles Stanley's book, 'How to Listen to God. He says further that "God does not say anything unless it's important and worth remembering." Psalm 85:8 says " I will hear what God the Lord will speak for He will speak peace to this people." I believe the Holy Spirit prompts us to use kind, gentle words. The Lord's tender and quiet nature is so needed in our world, and God's people can do this. If the world can't see these qualities in us, we have "missed the mark" in carrying His message. If they see nothing different about us, they have no reason to believe we have anything to offer them. We are carriers of His Gospel Message to speak peace and be carriers of His peace.

I look back into my long journey with the Lord, and know that God has spoken to me from many avenues; primarily from the Bible and God-loving people. He has spoken volumes through my own personal circumstances. We must be sensitive in sharing our thoughts, for God may be delivering a message to our listener. I pray that our words and the way we live always speak God's peace, and plants seeds of His love in each heart we touch.

"Be Not Dismayed"

Sometimes, we lie shattered and bewildered in the wake of life's trials. Our earthly journeys, at times, are devastating losses that break our hearts: a baby stillborn, a retiree's life cut short, goals set aside by injury, a parent dies, or a young life sentenced to death by disease. How do we understand? We can't, but must accept life by faith. We trust the wisdom of God's heart. We are earth bound, but here we're preparing for heaven's eternity. In Luke 22:31 Jesus warned Peter, "Simon, Simon, Satan has asked for you ..." Jesus could have said, "Peter, run for your life for Satan is after you. Instead, Jesus said calmly, "I have prayed that your faith won't fail..." He said to Peter, "Just trust me as you go through this time." Jesus even gave him a reason, "...it's to help your brothers be stronger...." Then our testing can be for someone else's benefit? I guess so. Trials are not to destroy us, but to make us stronger. Jesus warns us. "In the world you will have tribulations, but be of good cheer ..." John 16:33. He reminds us that He has overcome – and in the end for a Christian is victory. "Be not dismayed for I am your God..." Isaiah 4:10.

God So Loved

God so loved the world,
He loved mankind so much,
that He gave His only Son,
He gave His Son for us.

Christ came to die for us,
died for all our sin,
then from the grave He came
forth to live again.

God's love is real,
on this love we can depend.
He loved us all so very much
it's hard to comprehend.

His Round Trip

Each year we read the Baby's story; we travel with the shepherds to the birthplace. There we find God's greatest gift, and a great star leading others to Him. We ask why not a palace, a grand temple, but instead God chose a stable. "Praise the Lord. Let everything that has breath praise the Lord." Psalm 150:1 & 6. I've also wondered why God chose a stable for His Son, but then I remembered Grandpa's old barn. It was a sanctuary of sorts, quiet, dim with muted sounds, soft hay underfoot, and the odor of animals and old seasoned wood, an aura I've never forgotten. Then one day I reasoned why God chose a stable instead of a castle; it shows us that we can create something beautiful and wonderful in life under the toughest surroundings, if our Savior abides within us.

We celebrate with lights; God used His own light to decorate that night with a bright, twinkling star. He lights our world with the sun's brightness; He colors the four seasons, brings spring's new life, and gives us people and animals to love. Jesus came, He lived. He ministered to people. He died. He was buried. He arose from the grave. He ascended back to the Father. "Bless the Lord, 0 my soul, and all that is in me, bless His holy name..." His round trip was complete.

Far Away

Jesus returned to heaven, but He also dwells within us as the Holy Spirit. Once I experienced something as a teacher of a four-year-old that I've never forgotten. A little girl happy and energetic, sang loudly with us about going to God's House on Sunday morning. All was well until her grandmother died, and she was told that Grandma had gone to God's House to live. From that day she cried every Sunday morning. I asked her why she was so sad. She said, "I've looked everywhere for Grandma and she's not here, and I'm not coming back to God's House anymore." We never know how a child processes what we say to them.

I wonder how many adults feel the same way when they come to church and don't feel God's presence among us. God is invisible, yet He is among us for He dwells in believers; someday we will understand the phenomenon of this. John the Baptist's burning desire was to proclaim the great revelation God had given him, and one day he recognized Jesus as the long awaited Messiah and loudly proclaimed, "Behold, the Lamb of God who takes away the sin of the world." We can't see Jesus today, nor can we see heaven, but as His children we know He dwells in us for we feel His presence within.

Two Events

Most of you will not remember October 4, 1957, when the Soviet Union launched Sputnik 1, the world's first beach-ball-sized satellite. I remember the news of it flashing around the world. This changed history, sent technology into a frenzy that filled us with fear and hope. Today, we live with its reality of benefits and also its dark dangers. It's a milestone in history, while there is another event many years prior, which happened in obscurity, the birth of Jesus, God's Son. The shepherds spread the news by mouth! Yet no other event, past or present, has changed the course of history more than His birth. Today we still read of the announcement in the gospels and celebrate that birth and live by how it changed our world.

Just in my lifetime I've seen the advent of penicillin, the conquer of polio, propellers to jets, television, the split of the atom, conquering of space, a walk on the moon, search of outer space, miracle medical procedures, computer technology, on and on great world changes in history. Yet nothing can eclipse that quiet birth in the little town of Bethlehem. We still spread this news, not just by mouth, but modern technology. Today the entire world knows of His birth, his death, burial and resurrection for He is God's son, and someday He will return.

Loves' Dove

In reading the four gospels describing the baptism of Jesus, I became fascinated with each author's view of the Dove. Read, Matthew 3:13-17, Mark 1:9-11, Luke 3:21-13 and John 1:29-32. John the Baptist gave this testimony of baptizing Jesus, "I saw the Spirit come down from heaven as a dove and remained on Him... I have seen and I testify that this is the Son of God." John baptized Jesus so Jesus could identify with sinners, though sinless Himself. The voice of God from heaven was divine acknowledgement of Jesus as His Son and the Dove as the Holy Spirit. The voice from heaven was for the benefit of others, not for Jesus. This plainly reveals the Trinity, the Father's voice from heaven, Jesus the son of God, and the Holy Spirit as a Dove. God's love dwells in each believer, and remains within each believer. In scripture the dove is a symbol of an acceptable sacrifice because of its innocence. At Jesus' baptism the Holy Spirit descended from heaven, proclaiming the Father's love for His Son, whose life was to be sacrificed for the sin of humanity.

Now I know why a dove was such a special bird to my Grandfather who never raised a gun on a dove, though he hunted and defended his farm land. A man who could barely read, knew the dove as a symbol of God's love.

Handmade

"For we are God's own workmanship" Ephesians 1:9-10. This verse says we are "Made in Jesus Christ." God has a plan, a blueprint for each of His own redeemed by the blood of the Lamb. We walk through life under His construction as He fashions us to fit His plan. God sees us moving through the refining process. Millie Stamm tells in one of her books about a Mr. Borglum, who sculpted in marble the South Dakota Rushmore Monument, and then he sculpted the head of Lincoln in our nation's capitol. His cleaning woman once asked, "How did you know Lincoln's head was in that block of stone? God sees us in our raw block of humanity also, and knows that each believer can be sculpted according to His plan for each of us.

Sometimes when I stare at a white canvas, I see the image I want to paint. After sketching, painting and shading, the likeness appears. Our Lord molds us, and polishes us to grow into His plan. Some people mold easily, but most take patience and many do-overs to reach a dim likeness of what He wants us to be. God calls us, guides ud, and leads us into service. Whatever He has led you to do is His plan for you, serve Him faithfully for you are created unto Jesus Christ for your place in life.

Happy Masks

It's been said, "The radiance of a Christian is not a mask." It's inner happiness showing on the faces of those who live in complete trust in Christ." I'd never thought of my countenance being a witness, but it is the first thing someone sees of me. Though our hearts may be heavy or walking a rough road, but the Lord's joy fills our hearts so that it's visible to others. The face of Stephen had a great effect on Paul. In fact, I'm sure Stephen's face haunted Paul. Act 6:15, "And all who sat in the council, looked steadfastly at him, saw his face as the face of an angel." While they stoned him in Acts 7:54-58, "they were cut to the heart…" Stephen's expression of devotion was a face Paul could not forget. This one face helped change a man that God later greatly used in building His earthly kingdom. After Paul's conversion God used him to be the greatest leader in spreading the gospel and building churches in the Gentile world. Paul was a special vessel, and we must be eternally thankful for it was through Paul's work that we have the gospel today.

Our faces speak to others. Lives devoted to the Lord show in our lifestyles, in our homes, at our work places, or wherever we are. We have an awesome responsibility of showing God's love for we are always on display.

The Tug

My Uncle Jay, older than I, enjoyed entertaining me with funny stories. I call them my "cotton patch stories." One tale was of a jack rabbit flying a kite. I asked, "What's a kite?" He said, "Well, someday soon we'll make one and I'll show you." Long story short, I watched him build a kite with sticks, paper, string, and old rags for the tail. He got the kite up in the air, and I could hardly believe what I was seeing. He let me hold the cross-stick and feel the movement of the wind tugging the kite. I asked, "Is that God pulling on my kite? Somehow, those words had a profound effect on him, for in his lifetime he often mentioned God's tug on our lives. There are no kite stories in the Bible, but every time I read Psalm 139 verse 5 says, "You hedge me in behind and before; You laid your hand upon me. Such knowledge is too wonderful for me - it's too lofty for me to attain." In these words I sense God over us and feeling His tug keeping us close to Him. His hedge guards and cautions us. As Uncle Jay never forgot my childlike question, neither will we ever forget that special tug on my heart strings when He called to me and redeemed me setting me on track for eternal life. That tug is real when He calls unto each of us.

His Quiet Presence

Sometimes quietness is loud. Have you ever sat alone in a house that's home to you and hear the quietness beat its drums in your heart. The silence can be full and rich; it can be filled with memories or like a voice pondering your relationship with the Savior. Psalm 46: 10. "Be still and know that I am God I will be exalted in the earth." When a family member is gravely ill, and you sit by day after day, feeling as if your soul is parched - just know He is there. Whatever your circumstances, you will meet God over and over for He is with you. He abides within and in your thoughts as you walk with Him. Hear the silence of your heart; that is your heavenly Father comforting you. David certainly understood, for He speaks of it in prayer in Psalms 42 and 43. The phrase that caught my eye that I could relate to was 42: 8. "The Lord by day directs me and at night His song is with me..." I have heard His song in the night, and nothing is more precious that the presence of the Lord in the darkness of night when sleep will not come. When we struggle in the night, we can know God is right there with you. Let's pray often for those is our midst living alone, who experience dark nights. Our Lord is close, just be still, feel His Presence, and hear His voice.

Wait With Patience

How do we wait with patience? It's not easy. Waiting is not for us. Even James 1:3 says "...the trying of your faith works patience in us." Life is full of frustrations, even as grownups we can think childishly. We learn early in life that we can't have everything, and these are hard basic lessons to learn. Trials catch us off guard for we expect life to go our way, but problems can stretch our faith to the point of impatience. Learning to wait for God has a timing of His own. While we wait we experience God's care, and see His hand in ways about us. Though we don't like waiting, patience is learned obedience. Have you ever noticed when you are tired, hungry, or angry that pride raises its ugly head and lashes out. It is then, it's hard to calm your thoughts and have patience. We should be especially mindful of these moments, Psalm 40: 1 "I waited patiently for the Lord, and He inclined unto me, and heard my cry." Sometimes we see God's hand at work, sometimes not, but just know God is working for we can trust Him. Remember, most assets come to us after a period of waiting, so the most important thing is don't stop trusting, just wait for Him in His time.

I Can See Him

Of course, no one has ever seen God, but God made Himself visible in His Son. Jesus said to Philip, "...he who has seen Me has seen the Father ..." John 14:9. We've tried in many ways to unveil Him with paintings, images, books, songs, and music, but to me nothing reveals Him more than nature itself. I look at summer flowers and see God. I see Him in the eyes of my black and white cat. At every sunrise He declares each new day, the seasons change and new life comes each spring. This fills me with His peace. As God's child I sense His inner presence, and in medicine miracles I see the hand of the Great Physician. Rainbows show His everlasting promises. He gives us cherished hours with loved ones, and over my lifetime has showered me with His mercy and goodness in many ways. He is my Shepherd in the valley. I see Him in the eyes of my own loved ones. I feel His presence in my need, and though I cannot fully comprehend the fullness of His being, and though He is not visible to my eyes, He is in plain view of my heart. I see Him in mountains of the West, tall stately trees, and flowers nestled at my feet, and when I look up in prayer, I see Him as Creator, my Redeemer and my loving Father.

An Inspiration

I've just finished reading Billy Graham's Hope for the Troubled Heart, and I highly recommend it. It's an easy read, and written in a way as if he is seated right there in conversation with you. Its theme is finding God in the midst of problems that many consider hopeless. It's so down-to-earth in Billy Graham style, a farm boy from North Carolina who God has used to draw the world to Him for seven generations. The last chapters touched my heart about Heaven, it made me more aware of keeping my family house in order, so I can know we'll all be together in Heaven. Psalms 116:15 "Precious in the sight of the Lord is the death of His saints." We don't understand it, and Billy Graham admits he does not either, but we know death is a departure. Jesus said, "I go to prepare a place..." I quote Billy Graham, "Because Christ rose from the grave, we know there is life after death...." If there's anything that makes Heaven more real and precious to us is the fact that we have loved ones there now. That makes it home to us also. It's the ones residing inside with us that makes the house a home. You can go back to any old home site, and it's not the same, because the ones we loved are no longer there. Heaven's charm is because Christ, our Redeemer and our loved ones are there with us.

Cherished Memories

One of God's greatest gifts to mankind is our ability to remember, knowing God has forgiven us of our sin, never to remember again, but Satan will not let us forget. We each have plenty of hurts and disappointment in life that the Lord helps us overcome, and these make a treasure chest of priceless reminders. Our treasured memories of family, friends, and how the Lord has worked in our lives are also cherished forever. In Philippians 1:3, Paul said, "I thank my God for every remembrance..." Sometimes we lose a precious family member in death, a job lost, a friend, a home, or some other life changing event, it's then we look down the lonely road of recovery and find the Shepherd of the Valley already there to walk with us, which leave us many memories. I once read of a precious memory held close by a mother whose little boy ran away from home. He packed his peanut butter sandwich and left, but at the park he met an old man seated on a bench, and old man's smile so captivated him that he returned home to tell his mother that he'd had lunch with God. Then she later heard that the old man returned to the Living Center and told them that he had never realized God was such a sweet, loving child. What is your precious memory of seeing God in others?

Open Doors

Don't you enjoy open doors? Open doors mean welcome, come on in to friends and family. Closed doors are okay too, but they mean privacy, security, or maybe fear and loneliness. At times shutting out the world is the only way to be alone with God. The disciples were all huddled together behind closed doors out of fear after the resurrection. John 20: 18-19 says "Mary Magdalene told the disciples that she had seen the Lord earlier in the day, then the same day at evening...doors were shut out of fear... Jesus came and stood in the midst of them and said, Peace be with you." Jesus did not need an open door He just appeared to offer peace for fear. John says to us over and over in his accounts of these appearances that the doors were barred. To Jesus all doors are open. His disciples had not comprehend the challenges Christ had left with them; they had no peace because of fear, so in John 14:27 Jesus had said to them, "Peace I leave with you...let not your heart be troubled, neither let it be afraid." They heard His words, but not comprehended. Whether we live behind closed doors or open doors, the latch is always open to Him.

Crosses – Crosses

Everywhere we look today we see crosses, gold, silver, wood, in churches, in homes, on cards, and on hills. To us crosses are symbols of love, but not in ancient Rome where it meant execution, a horrible death on a rocky hill. I'll share with you about a little silver cross I carry in my coin purse? It was given to me during a period of grief with a poem entitled, "A Cross in my Pocket" by Verna Thomas. It was given to me as a reminder of His peace and comfort. That little cross reminds me to whom I belong. II Corinthians 5:7 Paul tells us, "We live by faith not by sight." John 16:5-16 Jesus tells the apostles that He was leaving and they could not come with Him. He comforted them by telling them of someone He was sending to be with them while He was gone. He told them the Helper was the Holy Spirit who will dwell in the heart of every believer. He guides, comforts and teaches and makes His presence known to us as he leads our thoughts and opens and closes doors. He is God's Spirit dwelling in each of His children. Be sensitive to His presence. The little cross I carry is scratched and dulled by coins, but every time I open the purse, it's always there to remind to me of the price Jesus paid for me.

Christmas and Easter

Luke 23 tells the story of the Lord's crucifixion, Jesus said, "Father, forgive them" for He knew they were unknowingly fulfilling God's eternal plan. His forgiving heart uttered to the thief, "Today you will be with me in Paradise." Jesus reacts when the Spirit moves within us and we respond. He was never too busy or in too much pain, for while He hung there, He asked John to take care of His mother. Just breaths from death He had others on His mind. Hanging there, He felt the emotional sin weight of the world in His last moments. He felt abandoned, for even God, the Father turned away. At that moment Jesus was just a bleeding sacrifice for sin. Separation from the Father ran deep, as He was a dying sacrifice for our sin. There He became our Redeemer. Some probably thought, at last pain for Him is over, others said our troublemaker is gone, but His purpose was fulfilled in victory! After His two loving followers buried Him, there was a long wait of what... uncertainty, but SUNDAY CAME. The angel's message, "He is not here, but is risen." He is alive, we worship Him today. He was born to die. Christmas and Easter are both essential - they are tied together by love told to us in God's Holy Word.

Street Memories

....I visited my old neighborhood, a residential area of moderate homes of working people just west of downtown Oklahoma City. I remember neat homes, nice yards, sidewalks, tall shady trees, neighborhood markets, one car families, metro transportation, no school buses, and kids walking to school together. Families were known and respected, kids played safely all through the yards, front porches were for visiting while kids romped around together. Does this sound familiar? A few years ago I went back to see the neighborhood, and my heart sank at the sight of some houses half torn down, windows boarded up and abandoned. It had become a ghetto, a pathetic sight like a dirty old 'bag lady" no longer loved or cared for by anyone. I left the area with tears in my eyes and a hole in my heart. What memories a street can hold. A few years later I took another drive to that long-ago place and surprisingly I saw changes. Some dilapidated houses had been torn down, and a few new ones built, others looked restored or in some stage of restoration. These houses were homes again. It thrilled my heart to see lawns mowed, kids running and playing along shady sidewalks. I saw hope in progress. I saw resurrection. Streets can change, just as people can change. Darkness cannot thrive, when it is conquered by Light.

My Lord is Near

My life has been a blend
of many things.
I've wandered to and fro
from Him.

I've promised and bargained,
then promised Him again.
Many times
I've grieved and
disappointed Him but

He always says to me,
"My child, for you I care."
Never has He left me
My Lord is always near.

Jesus Will Return

"Now when Jesus had spoken these things, they watched...as a cloud received Him out of their sight. While they looked upward two men stood by dressed in white. They asked, why do you stand gazing up into the heavens? This SAME JESUS who was taken up from you will come back in like manner just as you saw Him go into the heavens." Acts 1:9-11. The disciples, nor have we, ever seen anything like the ascension. We see planes and rockets disappear up out of sight, but never a person as Jesus ascended. The men in white asked, "Why do you stand gazing up into the heavens?" Just as the disciples, we also have work to do, for Jesus is coming back, He will one day split the sky with a shout. We don't want to be among those left gazing up wondering what had just happened!

We must work, wait, and watch for His return. Every generation talks of His return. As a child with my grandparents looking up into the summer's fleecy clouds and blue sky, Grandma often said, "One day Jesus will return in a cloud just like that one!" So I've been looking for Him a long time. I never look at a sky that I don't think of Paul's account in I Thessalonians 4, of the anticipated wondrous event. 'Watch, for one day He'll return in the blink of an eye.

Heart is a Temple

This morning I read I Corinthians 3: 16 Paul's question, "Do you not know that you are the temple of God, and that the Spirit of God dwells in you?" When I think of it, I find it hard to envision my body as a temple, but that's exactly what Paul said - each believer is a Temple. God gave His Law to the people in detail, they read and memorized it, but did not live it. Jeremiah, a prophet tells us of God's plan in 24:6-7, "...I will give them a heart to know me...they will return to me with all their heart." But in reality they still did not serve Him. Jesus Himself said in Matthew 22:37-38 "Love the Lord your God with all your heart and with all your soul, and with all your mind. This is the first and greatest commandment." We believe in love, expressing love, receiving love, but first we must love our Savior. The Holy Spirit lives in us to be our Guide, our Comforter and Companion to help us. Jesus said in John 14:16-17 "...I will ask the Father, and He will give you a Counselor to be with you forever - the Spirit of Truth ...He will live with you and will be in you." He is the redeeming red string of salvation in all those walking closely with the Lord; the Holy Spirit's presence abides in the temple of each believing heart. He is our constant companion.

His Great Realization

A songwriter named Asaph, one of David's chief musicians wrote psalm 73 when he must have been in a real crisis of faith. In verse one He agrees that "truly God is good," but could not understand why God allowed the wicked to prosper, while living a mockery of God. This inequity frustrated him, and we still stumble over this issue. It seems those who live seemingly unaware of God prospers more than God's own people. Asaph had let this fact defeat him. In verse 13, "Surely I have kept my heart pure in vain..." for in the Old Testament people viewed life as getting paid back for their sinful ways. Job's friends also accused him. They assumed he had unconfessed sin. Verse 16 says, "When I tried to understand this, it is too painful to me." Life is filled with inequities, so Asaph finally "went into the sanctuary of God, then I understood." There in God's presence, God gave him a new prospective with understanding, he understood that someday all inequities will be judged and settled by God. Things we don't understand, we leave to God. As old Fanny Crosby song says, "We'll understand it all by and by." Fanny was blind, but God gave her great insight, so When we question life's circumstances, read Psalm 73.

Happiness and Joy

I often wonder why God gives me words from His heart almost every morning to share. I've learned to just write them, and make them available to others, then leave the rest to God's plan. I know the Lord uses them for within the past year I've received letters from Texas, Arkansas, Louisiana, and Colorado telling me that a friend or relative sent them, and then how much the words ministered to them. So, I keep writing. Each day my heart is touched with inner joy, though it's limited to what I can do as I've grown older. Right now I'm enjoying some little stray cats I feed everyday on my patio. They are a real blessing to me. To me this is happiness, but what happens when illness and hurts come? Does my joyful mood disappear? Paul tells us, "Rejoice in the Lord always, and again I say, Rejoice." Philippians 4:4. Happiness and joy are practically the same, but there is a difference. Happiness is the result of our daily routine, a new home or car, a friend's visit, vacation, etc. Joy is deep-seated and does not depend on circumstances. In fact, our joy bubbles within in the midst of chaos. True joy is simply the result of trusting God, for I speak from experience. Joy is beneath all circumstances, because joy is forever. "My joy may remain in you and that your joy may be full." John 15:11. Let's be happy daily.

Grandma's Apple Parable

"A word aptly spoken is like apples of gold in a setting of silver." Proverbs 25:11. This little verse is special to me. No one used by-words, as Grandma called them, but one day I overheard a neighbor farmer visiting with Grandpa near the barn. That man used a word I found interesting, so I stored it away for future use. Long story short - one day Grandma corrected me and hurt my feelings, so I stomped outside to the windmill, set my foot upon the first rung of the metal latter, then another, then another. I thought I was high, and I spit out my "special" word to the wind, not once but three times. The sound sailed through the air, but those words had hardly fallen from my lips when Grandma had me by my dress tail and down I came. We flew across the yard like Dorothy flying in the wind. My feet hardly touched the ground. I could almost taste the soap or something worse. Instead, she sat me in a chair at the kitchen table, handed me a bright red apple from the glass bowel on the table. With tears I looked at the apple, when she said, "Good words are like clean apples in a crystal bowl. Bad words are like rotten apples." She said my life was on display in a crystal bowl. I grasp her idea and never forgot it. Later I found those words in the Bible. She was a wise Grandmother.

The Look

Reading Luke 22 this week I came across the Lord's conversation with Peter. At the Last Supper Jesus made the statement that one would betray Him, and this brought the subject of who among them would do such a thing. Indignant Peter thought he was the bravest and most devoted, but Jesus said, "Simon, Simon, Satan has asked to sift you...Oh, Peter, I tell you before the rooster crows today, you will deny three time that you even know me." I'm sure Peter's head bowed, thinking, "No, way, Lord." You know the story. Peter truly did disown Jesus three times, then "...the rooster crowed. The Lord turned and 'looked' straight at Peter..." Peter remembered and went outside and wept bitterly. I also remember my Grandma's silent 'look,' for those steel blue eyes spoke volumes to me. I knew I needed an attitude change. No words were necessary, her "look" said it all. We probably deny our Lord many times and don't admit it .Anytime we fail to speak up for Him, we deny Him. Mark 8:38 is a sobering scripture. "If anyone is ashamed of Me and My words ...the Son of Man will be ashamed of him when he comes into my Father's glory ..." Our salvation is certain, but do we ever realize a 'look ' of disappointment in His eyes? That's truly something to think about, and sincerely ask ourselves each day, "Lord, have I denied You today."

Our Praise to Him

Psalm 145 is a hymn of praise expressing faith to glorify the greatness of God. "Great is the Lord, and greatly to be praised..." The psalmist goes on to praise Him for mighty works, His glory, His goodness, great compassion, His care and His righteousness...all available to us. Sitting on the patio in the quietness of morning, I read this wonderful psalm of praise and realized that nature testifies of God's love. Nature supplies our needs, the sunshine and rains refreshes the earth, the mountains, streams, plains and deserts all testify of His handiwork. God's love is revealed even in the cursed ground of thorns and thistles. I hear a bird sing, watch a hummingbird sip nectar, or a butterfly lifts from bloom to bloom I think of God. When I see these I often think of Moses asking God to show him His glory, which God does in Exodus 33:18-19. What we see all around is God's glory, even in sickness, death, and other devises of Satan; he wants us to see God as austere and a severe judge, but Jesus came to show us God is Love in human form. "When you have seen me, you have seen God the Father." John 14:8-9. Just look around and see Him in loving Christians, faces of children, joys of nature and give thanks and praise to His Holy Name.

Your Choice

Covetousness is the desire of the natural eyes, wanting everything we see bigger, better and more of everything. Covetousness is the opposite of contentment. If a person cannot be satisfied with all the material things in which they've been blessed, their prayer should be, "Lord, show me contentment in You and not in what the world says I need." God wants us to have goals and He helps us attain our desires, but not to the point of greed. Jesus warns us, "Take heed and beware of covetousness for a man's life consist not in the abundance of the things he possesses." Luke 12: 15. We daily see greed increasing in people daily, even small children and especially teenagers wanting and demanding everything they see – never satisfied. The root of this ravenous craving for 'things' is growing in us.

Christians must be a light showing God's preserving contentment. One of God's basic requests is, "Thou Shall not covet..." Exodus 20:17. Jesus has the solution for greed. He said, "Seek the Kingdom of God and all these things will be added to you." Let us pray for contentment in our own lives, to show the world that happiness and contentment do not come from 'things', but from a deeper contentment found in the Christian values of life. Jesus being the basic source of contentment.

Joy Misplaced

Many things can rob our joy, but Jesus said in John 15, "These things I have spoken to you, that My joy may remain in you, and that your joy may be full." I read Proverbs 8 this morning, and every verse is a jewel. Read and listen as Wisdom speaks. God's wisdom is pictured even before He created the world. Notice verses. 22-23, "The Lord brought me forth as the first of His works. I was appointed from eternity from the beginning, before the world began"...verse 27, "I was there when He set the heavens in place..." verse 30-31, "Then I was the craftsman at His side, ...I was filled with delight day after day, rejoicing in His presence, rejoicing in His whole world and delighting in mankind." The Lord provides wisdom to rejoice in our souls, and gives comforts of home and family, livelihoods and talents to pursue bringing us joy. Don't let your "ordinary" of life become dull, rejoice in God's provision. In verse 30 Wisdom said, "...I was filled with delight day after day, rejoicing always in His presence." In verses 33-34 Wisdom gives us good advice, "Listen to my instruction and be wise; do not ignore it. Blessed is the man who listens to me..." When we get discouraged, assess what we have in Christ, and remember our Lord's words, "My joy is forever."

I Call Him Father

This week after I'd finished reading the Song of Solomon in my quiet time, I read an article entitled Lover of My Soul, by Joni Eareckson Tada. Joni said, "Her favorite approach to God when she prays is 'Lover of my Soul.' Occasionally, I talk to Him as my elder Brother; when spiritually attacked, I go to Him as 'Captain of my Soul,' as my 'Friend' I pour out my soul to Him, but my favorite is 'Lover of my Soul...'" Her beautiful article made me think of my own vision of God. To me He is always, "Father." As a young teenager, one of the first things I thought when I raised from the altar was now I have a Father who will never leave me. He must love all His names, but He is always there however we address Him. I've written many times of prayer, because I know of no other thing in our lives that's more important than prayer. As we look ahead each day, ask Him to fill your eyes with visions of hope, and enrich your courage and boldness, and Help us not run ahead or lag too far behind of Him, but walk with His steps. Ask for a fresh anointing of His Spirit each day, and remain steady with a sense of assurance in belonging to your Father.

Prayer for Others

When someone says, "Please pray for me." I ask the Lord to intervene in their wellbeing and supply their needs. God tells of His care all through His word, and in John 17: 17 Jesus Himself prayed for His children's rest. Matthew 11:28 "Come to Me, all you who labor and are heavy laden, and I will give you rest." When emotionally weak and our strength is waning, David said in Psalm 4:1, "You have relieved me in my distress. Have mercy on me and hear my prayer." Psalm 18:6 is a favorite of mine, "In my distress I called upon the Lord and cried out to my God. He heard my voice from His temple, my cry came before Him even to His ears." Often we are depleted by our own doing, read Proverbs 2:3-6 "If you cry out for discernment, then you will find knowledge of God. For the Lord gives wisdom, from His mouth comes knowledge and understanding." My all-time favorite answer for our needs is Philippians 4:5-6. "Don 't worry about anything, but in everything by prayer and thanksgiving, let your requests be made known to God, and the peace of God, which surpasses all understand will guard your hearts and minds through Jesus Church our Lord."

What if?

Our 'what if' can be frightening words. We imagine every conceivable bad thing that might happen to us, and ninety-nine percent of the time none of our negative worries ever happen. These 'what ifs' should call us to prayer. Satan tries his 'doom and gloom' to weaken us, but every time we must remember God's faithfulness. Read Lamentations 3:22-23; Jeremiah remembered his afflictions, yet he felt hope; he confessed God's faithfulness. "Through the Lord's mercies we are not consumed, because His compassion fails not. They are new every morning. Great is Your faithfulness." David's psalm of praise in Psalm 103: 1-4 "Bless the Lord, O my soul,... and forget not all His benefits; who forgets all our iniquities, who heals our diseases, who redeems our lives from destruction, who shows us loving kindness and tender mercies." Each new day not only contains His mercies, but His new challenges and opportunities. Let's kick Satan off to the sideline with his bag of "what ifs," for we have too many benefits being God's children to let Satan disturb us. Praise the Lord each morning and Satan flees for he cannot stand our praises to God.

Living Stones

This morning I read I Peter 2:4-5, where Peter refers to us as "living stones" This made me wonder what it means to build the kingdom. Jesus is the Chief Cornerstone per Isaiah 28:16. A cornerstone is the foundational stone, the anchor, an important part of any building. With no knowledge of building, I can see that all measurements must be square with that stone. I Kings 6:7, "In building the temple only blocks dressed at the quarry were used, and no hammer, chisel or any other iron tool was heard at the temple while it was being built." Each stone cut and chiseled was perfectly hewn ahead of time for its place in the temple plan. Some require cutting and refining to fit in designated places. Often we whine and even rebel when difficulties come to us, yet I am convinced that our trials are refining us today in life's quarry. A man seeking work asked, "What are you doing to that stone?" The workman pointed upward and replied, "You see that opening way up there in the design close to the top? Well, I am shaping this stone down here so that it fits perfectly up there." I see, we, as living stones, are being uniquely shaped down here, so we will fit in the place God has planned for us up there. This is a visual picture of how I see us as living stones.

Sheltering Love

My heart is touched when I read, "Be merciful to me, O God, be merciful to me! For my soul trusts in You, and in the shadow of Your wings I will make my refuge, until these calamities have passed by." Psalm 57:1. God's love is sheltering us as we read His holy words. The answer to being a secure Christian through whatever touches our lives, read this note of encouragement from Helen Steiner Rice. "God, teach me to be patient to wait on You when my way is unknown, for God has a quiet peace waiting for me near His heart. When we feel God's comfort, it's because we are resting in His arms. David called this place a refuge and a fortress; in fear its safety, in sorrow its comfort, and in distress its security." Psalm 61:2-4 says, "When my heart is overwhelmed, lead me to the Rock that is higher than I. For You have been a shelter for me. I will trust in the shelter of Your wings." Even when in the hot sunshine, and suddenly a cloud crosses your path like an oasis, you feel its coolness like the Lord is refreshing you. Even in night shadows, "When I remember You on my bed, I meditate on You in the night watches...Because You are my help..." Psalm 63:6-7. I think it's then He has us emotionally tucked away in His sheltering arms.

Which Way is Home?

Jesus said in John 14: "I go to prepare a place for you." Where did He have to go? Golgotha was the place and on the cross He paid the bounty for all our sins. His words, "It is finished!" were words that allowed God to rip apart the temple veil to give us access to Him. His resurrection from the grave was the crowning victory. The old hymn says "It is sweet to know as onward we go, the way of the cross leads home." God set two ways before us, "the narrow gate and the broad gate that leads to destruction...narrow is the gate and it's difficult but leads to life, and few will find it." Matthew 7:13-14. When He beckons to each of us at a crossroad in life, we choose to enter either a narrow gate, or a wide, bright, glitzy highway, which actually leads to destruction in the end. It's ours to choose to follow Him or not. Christianity is God's search for those who will believe. Today, some say there are many ways to God, but in truth there is only one way, and you will enter through this narrow gate, and that gate is Jesus. He says, "I am the Way...and no one comes to God, except through me." John 14:6. There is only one way. Matthew 10:38 tells us that Jesus is the Door and He invites all to enter.

Treasures

Today—
Right here now,
all around is a special place.
There may be troubled spots,
it seems to come to all,
but look again upon your path—
it may be bordered with patience
and help from someone else's hand.
Showers of blessing come from above,
through hearts you know and love.
So look around—
and you may find
sparkling jewels within your reach
of kindness and love.

What "Wonders" Lie Ahead?

There is a distinct relationship between today and tomorrow. I examined myself for how much tomorrow rules my today, and found I place a lot of emphasis on tomorrow. I read a quote, "Tomorrow's miracles begin with today's consecration." The writer referred to Joshua's instructions to the Israelite people standing on the bank of the Jordan River on the opposite side of the Promised Land. In Joshua 3:5 Joshua instructed them, "Consecrate yourselves today, for tomorrow God will do wonders among you." Consecration is the yielding of ourselves to God, His plan and purpose. It's an outward and inward cleansing for total commitment to Him. We relinquish our today's plans in order for Him to do the "the wonders" in our lives tomorrow. The Lord needs each of us to commit ourselves to seeking His will.

Hear Paul saying in Philippians 3:13, "the one thing I do, forgetting those things which are behind, I reach forward to those things which .are ahead..." If anyone ever had a past to haunt them, it's Paul, so let's put everything that's happened behind us, and consecrate on the "wonders" of what God can bring to our lives today.

Blessings to Share

Sitting on the patio today looking over the yard I know personally the hours of work invested in it. Now as I see my landscaped yard, I remember Grandma's yard. I bought most of my plants and nurtured them into the beauties they are today, but Grandma's green thumb flowers came from the sharing of others. There was no money to buy plants, so neighbors shared and divided so all could have beautiful flowers. I remember Irene's plants blooming from a little twig, Florene's rose from a fresh cutting, Ruby's rose moss scattered at our feet, Ethel's hollyhocks, while Aunt Mandy lilacs, given long before I was born, still smelled heavenly. The ground covered moss Grandma carried from Texas to Indian Territory when they moved in a covered wagon to Oklahoma in 1904. Most of Grandma's flowers came from gifted seeds, a shared cutting or twig. In my own yard I am blessed by Betty's day lilies and iris, and a beautiful vine given to me from my friend Carolyn. This gives my garden warmth and character for each plant has a history. This all reminds me of Paul's letter to Timothy in I Timothy 6:18, "Let them do good, that they be rich in good works, ready to give, willing to share." Of course, Paul was speaking of other matters, but the giving-sharing principle is the same.

When Bad Times Strike

Today there is much pain and cruelty in the world, and the media coverage is so quick we hear every gruesome detail. Our Bible and our history are filled with man's battle with all forms of evil, but this is reality in the devil's kingdom. Distress touches all of us, for we see firsthand the gambit of broken lives from all sorts of evil. I always think of Job when I hear of brokenness in the lives of people and like Job I cannot understand. Job could have cried, "Why me?" and fell apart, but instead he must have said I don't understand, but I know "God is wise in heart and mighty in strength..." Though he did not understand, he trusted God Almighty. Remember Paul pleaded for God to remove his physical problem, but God told him, "My grace is sufficient..." At times God does not remove our problems, He strengthens our faith and walks with us through it. God designed us to need each other. Read in Galatians 6:2 he tells us to "Bear one another's burdens..." Several years ago I was in the hospital, when a big hand reached for mine, I looked up into the eyes of my cousin, one that I had led to the Lord way back when we were teenagers. We don't often see each other, but my soul rejoice when I saw him and heard his prayer for me. The Lord blessed and strengthened me through him.

Even There

I love it when the Lord points out special words to me. Today I read again Psalm 139 and verses 9 and 10 took on new meaning, "If I take the wings of the morning and dwell in the uttermost parts of the sea; even there Your hand leads me and Your right hand holds me." I realize as each day passes I'm in His sight all the way. He is our Omnipotent companion who sees and knows – it's like He holds us in His hand of love. "Even there" may be a place where we carelessly drift out of His will, but still He gently leads and holds us with a hand of love. Just knowing He is ever present in our lives leads us back to him and gives us ultimate security in spite of our wayward actions.

As I begin each day I picture myself being held by His right hand. I pray, Lord, give me courage and discernment if I find myself 'even there' where I did not intend to go. Joshua also heard Him in chapter 1:9 "Have I not commanded you! Be strong and of good courage, do not be afraid, nor be dismayed, for the Lord your God is there with you wherever you go." Each day let us picture ourselves being held by His right hand and led by His ever present guiding hand wherever we find ourselves.

Self Inventory

At the beginning of each day ask the Lord to be your guide. Each beginning is the time to 'wipe the slate clean' at a new starting place. Ask yourself some pertinent questions every so often; take inventory of your time and personality status, for bad habits can easily creep into our lives. Ask whom do I need to forgive? From whom or what forgiveness do I need to seek? What burdens of tension or guilt do I need to shed? What contradictions and habits do I need to correct? What hurts and grudges do I needlessly hold tightly? What commitments did I fail to keep and need to complete? What defeats do I battle? What is robbing me of my time? What disappointments are robbing me of my joy?

Take an honest inventory regularly to shed light on the scene. John 8:12 "I am the Light of the world. He who follows Me shall not walk in darkness, but have the light of life." His light exposes faults in my character. I pray for a constant flow from His artesian power filling me with eternal grace, with guidance in every decision, and be Lord of all I do and say.

Jesus is our Guest

I read this morning in Revelation 3 about Jesus standing at our door knocking. Of course, I believe this is referring to accepting Christ as our Savior, but when I read those words again today I realized anew that when we have invited Him into our lives He is our permanent guest. He knocked and waited for us to ask Him in. We willingly opened our door to Him and He entered to live with us. He hears all our discussions, our future plans, and He sees when we are disgruntled and disagreeable. I even envision Him with us listening to our conversations, the games we play, even our arguments and discussions completely ignoring His presence. He sees us in times of happiness, in sickness, in deceit, and in our rush leaving no time to enjoy the intimacy of His presence.

When I actually envisioned Him as a constant guest in my home I looked around and I saw a hundred horrid ways in my life that I need to change in order to be a proper hostess to my Guest. I saw neglect, pushing Him aside out of my way, rushing passed Him with no thought of His presence and not even heeding His voice when He speaks. Oh, I pray, "Lord forgive me, help me be a better listener, and to take the time to rest quietly with You, so I can hear your whispers in my heart.

Already in Place

There are many Bible verses special to me, but one is exceptional, because it came to me in an unusual way. "Fear not for I am with you. Be not dismayed for I am your God; I will strengthen you, I will help you, I will uphold you by my right hand of righteousness." Isaiah 41:10.

This verse was given to me in a rare dream long before I knew I had any need of it. I don't have the space to tell the story in detail of the dream, but during the dream my husband was missing and these words were etched in my heart as I searched for him. This verse was special to me for some reason, but not until six months later did these words have a full and profound meaning to me— when my husband of thirty-eight years died suddenly. From that moment these words have throbbed in my heart over and over when I need them.

I feared being alone, "Fear not for I am with you." I doubted, "Don't be dismayed by this for I am your God." When I was weak He strengthened me, and when I said, "But Lord I can't..." these embedded words came, "I will help you, I will uphold you with the right hand of My righteousness." He talked to me through these words throughout the days, months and years that followed.

I thought at times I could not go on, but He empowered me each day with confidence to do what I had to do. Never was the way too dark and cold that I could not feel the warmth of His presence; never was the time when I did not feel His everlasting arms holding me close.

I truly believe our Shepherd walks daily with us over the rocks and hard places helping all those who love and serve Him. He has no favorites; His hand of love and guidance is there whenever or wherever we need Him. His extended hand is there in any darkness you might be walking through right now. Of course, He also walks with us in the sunshine for He is our God and loves our fellowship. His presence is real, so spend some quiet time with Him each day.

A Completed Life

There comes that day
when a life, filled
with the energy and beauty
of a flower,
dies by the winds of time.
Its spirit takes flight to bring
this completed life
to its heavenly home,
while the body awaits
here in its resting place
for the resurrection spring.
A tiny spark
of faith is planted here
like a withered seed
beneath the ground,
just resting there
waiting to come forth
and rise
at God's trumpet sound.

CONTENTS

A Bible Hero 10
A Fragrant Life 113
A God-Honored Woman 168
A Line in the Sand 52
A Mosaic Snapshot 163
A Rainbow Memory 71
A Refreshed Vision 146
A Red Carpet 152
All Eyes Forward 83
Already in Place 216
Always There 171
An Empty Vessel 117
Angelic Signal 125
An Inspiration 187
Anna 28
Arc of Light 170
Attic Retreat 143

Beautiful Feet 110
Benchmarks, Great Church 29
Be Not Dismayed 175
Blessed is the Christian 123
Blessings to Share 211
Building Memories 91

Cherished Memories 188
Christmas and Easter 191
Cover With Love 132
Crosses-Crosses 190
Crown Him 73

Designer Creator 129
Devil Next Door 158
Doing my Part 122
Don't Hoard Blessings 141
Don't Let the Past Haunt 23

Each New Day 19
Even There 213
Eyes are Watching You 24

Faithful to the End 11
Far Away 178
First Thought in Morning 41
Floods and Rising Tides 120
For a Lifetime 111
Foundation in Darkness 139
Four Anchors 49
Four Magic Words 63
Freedom 103
Furnace of Affliction 54

Gideon's Story 151
God Does not Chit Chat 174
God is Faithful 155
God Loves Us as His Own 27
Godly Wisdom 173
God's Friend 46
God's Heart Desire 140
God's Leadership 13
God's Night Song 131

God's Picture 58
God's Power in our Lives 161
God's Quiet Voice 16
God's Space 159
God the Artist 92
Good Health Plan 137
Grandma's Apple Parable 198
Great Stabilizer 114

Handmade 181
Happiness and Joy 197
Happy in Spite of 86
Happy Masks 182
Hear the Silence 55
Heart is the Temple 195
Heart Treasure 57
Heavenly Radar 62
He Planned my Day 104
He is our Shield 25
Her Words of Wisdom 18
His Great Realization 196
His Presence 26
His Quiet Presence 184
His Round Trip 177
Hollyhock Seed 87
Hope is the Answer 68

I am a Branch 75
I am Here 93
I am with You 67
I Call Him Father 203
I can do it Myself 106
I can see Him 18l
I Found Ultimate Security 30
In God we Trust 95

Inspired Beauty 165

Jesus is our Guest 215
Jesus will Return 194
Joy in Life 148
Joy Misplaced 202
Just Words 154

Lead me – Guide me 65
Learn From David 32
Learned Attributes 87
Let Your Life be Sunshine 164
Light Available 14
Links in a Chain 78
Listen in Silent Moments 153
Listen to Hear My Voice 9
Listen to the Father 157
Living Stones 206
Love's Dove 180
Love's Fragrance 108

Magnify Him 133
Man in God's Image 44
Memorable Time 32
Modern Giants 172
Moments to Remember 169
More Precious than Gold 63
More Than Taste 59
My Own Worry 118
My Secret Place 37
My Shepherd 100
My View of me 142
Needed – a Guide 119
New Creatures 12

Old Age 61
Open Doors 189
Ordinary People 79
Our Comfy Ways 167
Our Constant Refuge 34
Our Creator 102
Our God Who Sees 20
Our Personal High Priest 136
Our Praise to Him 200

Paul says, I Know, I Know 124
Perfect Timing 162
Power Packed Words 130
Pray-Pray-Pray 82
Prayer for Others 204
Prayer Instructions 88
Prayer is Fruitful 156
Psalm Twenty-Three 15
Psalm's Soft Words 21

Rainbow Love 85
Rays of Hope 115
Real Storage 98
Red Light Patience 50
Rest in the Lord 116
Roll Away the Darkness 69

Sanctuary 150
Security Plus74
Self Inventory 214
Sheltering Love 207
Side by Side 126
Sin's Gulf – Love's Bridge 53
Soar on Wings 43

Something Priceless 134
Something Valuable to 35
Special Verbs 76
Special Vessel Just as I am 90
Spring's Returns 45
Stay Focused 70
Street Memories 192
Stewards of What? 121
Stress Alarm 189

The Calm of Inner Peace 127
The Little Sparrow 77
The Look199
The Lord of History 36
The Masks we Wear 147
The Small Stuff' 99
The Stable Rock 81
The Stone Man 109
The Tug 183
They Came – They Saw 145
Time Well Spent94
Times and Places 138
This can be a Good Day 107
This Day is all we Have 56
Today is Wonderful 135
Trials of our Faith 105
Two Events179

Unspoken Words 84

Wait with Patience 185
We Pray – We Wait 66
What Better Fortress 72
What Does it Take? 42

What if? 205
What is Trust? 38
What Road? 101
What Wonders LIe Ahead 210
What's Better than Rubies? 22
When Bad Times Strike 212
Which Way is Home? 208
Whose Plan? 41

Why do we Pray? 39
Will Never Cease 166
Wounded Pearl 47

Year Around Garden 149
Your Adversary 40
Your Choice 201

POEMS

Lover of My Soul 16
God's Blue Sky 32
God's Faithful Care 48
God's Way 64
My Jeweled Path 80
One-way Journey 96
Language of Love 112
Blessings 128
Prolific Vine 144
I Am Sure 160
God So Loved 176
My Lord is Near 193
Treasures 209
A Completed Life 218

Mary M. Chase

Mary M. Chase, born to Joel Richard and Rhoda Lee Shelton in Norman, Oklahoma in 1922.

At an early age she enjoyed exploring pasture land of the red sand hills, climbed sand rock boulders and played among blackjack oak trees and wild grape vines. She says she may be one of Oklahoma's first graffiti artist, for she scraped pictures and writings on all the big sand rock boulders found in the area. These natural surroundings created in her a love of God's handiwork, and is deeply founded in the Christian values of her Grandparents. Growing up experiencing both the Dust Bowl days and the Great Depression, her teenage years knew nothing but economic hard times. This made her a survivor at many junctures of life. Through grief she found solace in writing thoughts on paper; which resulted in college writing classes to develop this skill.

She has served as a docent at the National Cowboy and Western Heritage Museum since 1991. She is an artist in several mediums, an active, award winning poet in The Poetry Society of Oklahoma, and has sold several articles, essays and stories, authored six books, self-published poetry chapbooks, and one short novel Micah's Lamb.

Published Books

Mary's Garden
A life story about her search for "something" seeking passage through her teenage years resulting in victorious living of the young, troubled girl who grew up to become a great grandmother.
Copies available @ Amazon and book stores.

Rhody
A fictional book in part for young readers (12-14) about Mary's mother and her younger brother moving to Oklahoma with their family in a covered wagon in 1904. Copies available @ Amazon and book stores.

Fireside Embers
A collection of favorite stories recalled from a lifetime of paths and highways of her life.
Copies available @ Amazon and book stores.

Flashbacks of God at Work
A collection of stories of God at work in the lives of everyday Christian people. Out of print.

Melodies of Life in Poetry
A book of inspired poetry written mostly in free verse.
Copies available @ Amazon and book stores.

Jewels from His Treasury
A book on overcoming grief from personal experiences.
Copies available @ Amazon and book stores

Talking to You (a 2015 publishing date)
A book of meditations.
Copies available @ Amazon and book stores.

Made in the USA
Lexington, KY
24 October 2015